JAN 17 '95	DATE DUE		
SEP 29 1995			
MAR 18 1996			

THE AUTOBIOGRAPHY OF

MOTHER JONES

Edited by Mary Field Parton
Foreword by Clarence Darrow

Introduction and Bibliography
by Fred Thompson

Third Edition, Revised

DISCARDED

1980
Chicago

Charles H. Kerr Publishing Company
Published for the Illinois Labor History Society

LC 76-6584
PAPER ISBN 0-88286-013-5
CLOTH ISBN 0-88286-010-0

TABLE OF CONTENTS

LIST OF ILLUSTRATIONS

Some Dates in Mother Jones' Life

*Commission on Industrial Relations

Mother Jones with the Miners' Children

V

Mary (Mother) Jones; Terrence V. Powderly (standing), President of Knights of Labor; John P. White, President of United Mine Workers.
(From the Archives of Catholic University, Washington, D.C.)

Mother Jones with the steel strikers in 1919. At the left is Phillip Murray. Behind Mother Jones at the right is William Z. Foster.

Mother Jones Marching With The Children

VIII

INTRODUCTION

Mary Harris Jones wrote this account of her labor union activities when she was an old, old woman. By a few years she had missed the establishment of the first central body to serve the various local unions in an American city when it was founded in Philadelphia in 1827. She was to die, 1930, five years before the CIO was founded as the Committee for Industrial Organization, and she missed little in the development of the labor movement in between. She had backed various efforts to build more effective forms of labor solidarity. She had worked for the railroad shop unions that wanted to bargain as one unit, and the coal miners and metal miners who had early insisted on industrial union structure, one union for all crafts on the job.

Her memories summarize the long story of labor organization as much by the variety of her experiences as by her decades of involvement. She had made her living as a dressmaker, custom work on her own premises just as most handicrafts had been conducted in the colonial era. When she organized the housemaids in Scranton in 1901 she set up a union for an occupation that had not previously had one, and for workers in as close a personal relation to their employers as colonial craftsmen had been to theirs. No doubt both lots of employers insisted they had the good of their servants more at heart than any stranger coming in to make trouble between them. Where West Virginia or Colorado coal companies ruled as absolute monarchs she might as well in 1902 or 1913 have been facing the common law rule that prevailed until 1809 that it was against the law to seek an increase in wages by a "combination". In 1897 at the time of the Lattimer massacre she was on her way to visit a Utopian colony at Ruskin, Tennessee, and found, as workers had found in the 1840's, that it takes more than congregations of men and women of good will to give the working class a chance. She had seen successful union officers become officers of coal corporations. She had seen unions pressed to accept token gains and accomodate themselves to the views of the powerful, avoiding any expression of hostility toward the wages system and its free enterprise facade. She had known a textile president to explain that he would be cheating his stockholders if he paid his workers one penny more than he must, profitable starvelings that they were. She knew that under these arrangements workers got only what they had the organized power to get, and her life was devoted to enhancing that power.

Her book thus recapitulates a much longer working class experience. The main body of this book is a facsimile of the original 1925 Kerr edition, a completely undocumented record of an old woman's uncertain memories. For Kerr's 1972 edition I wrote an introduction intended primarily to help the reader find documented descriptions of the events in which she had been involved. This procedure confirmed and at times corrected her recollections. It proved useful both in class rooms and for those who dug labor history on their own. On the suggestion of some who used it the present introduction has been expanded to add detail to her story and offer a skeleton sketch of the growth of the labor movement in which she was involved.

Sources, alphabetically arranged, are listed at the end of this introduction and are also numbered to permit reference to them in the brief form (9:61) to mean page 61 of Brook's *Toil and Trouble* which is numbered 9. References to this book will be made as J:64 to mean the page number 64 in this facsimile of the 1925 edition.

Important new sources have been published since the 1972 edition. George McGovern expanded his 1953 doctoral dissertation on the 1913-1914 Colorado coal strike (as well as running for President) with the aid of Leonard Guttridge into the book *The Great Coalfield War* (36). George Suggs' *Colorado's War on Militant Unionism* (49) studies the Cripple Creek struggle of 1903-04. Dale Featherling's *Mother Jones the Miner's Angel* (21) is the most complete account of Mother Jones published to date. Lois C. McLean has kindly furnished important data from her still incomplete research for a definitive biography of Mother Jones, and reference to this correspondence is numbered 37-A.

The early unions of this country were local bodies of men who lived by the same craft as printer or carpenter or shoemaker. When they found they had to tie up production to get better pay they needed only that others who had their

iv

same skills and who lived nearby refuse to take their places. Early demands were for one's own craft only. In the 1830's workers raised social demands, as for free public schools and an end to imprisonment for debt, demands that concerned all workers and could be granted only by public authorities. For such objectives city trade councils were fostered. These often provided a common meeting place and library. They encouraged mutual aid in strikes and a concerted demand for a ten-hour day instead of working from sun-up to sun-down.

By 1860 when Mary Harris stopped teaching at the convent school in Monroe (J:11) canals and railroads had made it easier for workers to travel and compete with one another face to face, or for their products to reach distant markets and perhaps unwittingly break each other's strikes. The Civil War and its need for uniforms replaced custom-made shoes and clothes with factory products. Its armament needs replaced the village blacksmith with the technology of standardized interchangeable parts. The market became nationwide. Workers had to form nationwide unions for their crafts and in lagging response they did (55).

An outstanding national craft union in those days of stoves and ranges was that of the Iron Molders. In 1861 Mary Harris married George Jones, an iron molder, honored by this union at the time of his death in 1867 for his organizing work (44 and 21:5). William Sylvis, president of the Iron Molders had felt the need for a general labor movement to serve the working class as a whole. Todes (53) and Grossman (28) tell of Sylvis' efforts through the National Labor Union (1866-1872) to build a movement with the various city central bodies as major building blocks, thus focusing on the general labor concern rather than the aims of each specific craft.

The Knights of Labor, the Industrial Congress, the Industrial Brotherhood, were other responses to this need. In 1863 the Machinists and Blacksmiths had appointed a committee to sound out officers of other unions, and eight years later the call for the Industrial Congress was the result. Meanwhile in 1869 some Philadelphia garment cutters had formed a secret society, more a fraternal order in its early days than a union, and called it the Noble Order of the Knights of Labor (58). For years it grew slowly, and blossomed out as the first mass labor movement in America in the mid-eighties, with 702,000 members at its peak in 1886.

Terence V. Powderly became Grand Master Workman of the Knights and their chief spokesman. In her later years Mother Jones often stayed at his Washington home. He had first joined the Machinists and Blacksmiths in 1871, had organized in the Pittsburgh area for the Industrial Brotherhood, joined the Knights of Labor in 1876, bringing it the declaration of principles of the Brotherhood, and providing the typical motto that circled the Knight's seal "An injury to one is the concern of all". Years later in his book *The Path I Trod* (43) he wrote: "it was the intent of those who founded the Industrial Congress and later the Industrial Brotherhood to bring the scattered, weak and defenseless trade unions of the day into closer affiliation and cause the membership in each to devote time to the study of social, economic and political questions as well as those pertaining to their trade relations". (43:40) His description of how he came to join the Knights shows the protective secrecy of men fearful of the blacklist. A workmate had suggested that they meet to go to a labor lecture. "I presented myself at the designated place, accompanying my friend to a hall, and was mystified when we were ushered into a small room and told to wait. Soon a man wearing a black gown and mask came to question us". He wrote also "Women were not granted the right of membership until 1881". (43:45) This date and the early secrecy of the Knights jar with Mother Jones recollection (J:14) and with her 1915 testimony to the Commission on Industrial Relations where, speaking of the great railroad strike of 1877 she said: "The strike began in Martinsburg. . . it reached down to Pittsburgh and east to Scranton. I was in New York. I came down. I was a member of the Knights of Labor at the time, and some of the boys met me and asked me to stay with them and I did". (54:10619) Wives of railroad workers played an outstanding role in this the most important labor struggle of the seventies (8 and 10). Mother Jones' account (J:14) of a meeting in Louisville may have some reference to the brief-lived Industrial Association that met there in 1864, and some of her references to the Knights may be to other organizations; but then again who would have expected the coal miners' most noted organizer to be an old woman?

In 1881 the top officers of the trade unions formed the Federation of Organized Trade and Labor Unions of the United States and Canada on the model developed by British unions during their very conservative phase following the collapse of the Chartist insurgency. In it the carpenters initiated the proposal that on and after May 1, 1886 workers refuse to work more than eight hours. Widespread strikes occurred on that date but the event is most remembered for the bomb thrown by some unknown person into the meeting called to protest police brutality in Chicago's Haymarket (19 & J:17). The anti-union movement became a crusade. Union officials refused to speak up for those wrongly accused of responsibility for the bomb. The Knights had lost their big strike on the railroads and gave up their long strike in the Chicago packinghouses when many felt it was about won. In December 1886 the 1881 trade union federation turned all legislative and related functions over to the city and state federations to fit the apparent American political structure and adopted the new name American Federation of Labor. Its member unions tended to centralize control in their national officers, and these in turn ran the new AFL, for at its conventions the delegates from each national trade union had a vote for each hundred members while a delegate from a city or state federation, no matter how large, had only one vote. This plan reversed the National Labor Union and other attempts to build for wider working class solidarity. From 1886 to 1936 the AFL was the big trade union body in America, its guiding spirit Samuel Gompers of the Cigar Makers who presided over it to his death in 1924 (except for the one year 1894 when radical elements managed to replace him with McBride of the miners.) A major but unstated purpose of the AFL was to prevent trade union members from getting involved in any general working class organization.

The Knights wanted no quarrel with the national trade unions and would have welcomed a peace treaty that assured those unions their jurisdictions yet have permitted their members to join the Knights also as an expression of their wider working class concern, and, where towns were too small for a craft to maintain a local, bargain through the local mixed assemblies of the Knights (9:61). The Brewery Workers belonged to both AFL and the Knights until the AFL forbade this.

The United Mine Workers of America was formed in 1890 by a merger primarily of District 135 of the Knights and the National Union of Miners and Mine Laborers (1). The latter had been founded in 1882 with a scattered membership in West Virginia, Pennsylvania and the central states largely because the Knights were reluctant to attempt a national industrial structure until it did so with the formation of its District 135, nationwide, in 1886. These two groups did manage in that hectic year to meet jointly with operators in the central field and set wages to May 1887, but were not able to renew this arrangement. They could look back at such lost and bloody battles as the Hocking Valley strike of 1884 led by McBride of the Ohio State Miners' Union, and the hanging of the anthracite miners as alleged Molly Maguires (1) in the seventies, and the use of miners of one county to defeat their fellow workers in an adjoining county. The National Union favored AFL affiliation and the new UMWA joined it. The presence of this industry-wide union in a predominantly craft union federation created friction as Electrical Workers, Blacksmiths and Carpenters wanted to retain the few members of their crafts who worked in and around mines. The UMW neither wanted these skilled men to make separate contracts that would oblige them to keep on working when the miners struck, nor did it want strikes of one or two craftsmen to throw a hundred mine employees out of work as President Mitchell told the AFL convention in 1900 (25:87) with the result that the Scranton Declaration of the AFL granted the coal miners its one and only exception to its policy of craft dismemberment of industrial solidarity.

Mother Jones came to be so associated with these miners that she reflected their view of what a union needs to be. Different social outlooks accompanied the two types, craft union and industrial union, and these differences were vital at a time when the importation of workers with strange tongues was a customary way of keeping labor disorganized (2). The craft unions tended to confine membership to the friends and the ethnic groups of those running them, while the industrial unions wanted to unite all whom the employer had hired. The usually unspoken underlying assumptions differed too. The British model on which the AFL was based had developed at a time when popular belief and orthodox economics accepted the Wage Fund Theory. This reasoned that at any point in time there was just so much money available for paying wages and consequently the average wage was determined by dividing the number at work into the wages fund. Thus if some got more, others must get less. Another version ran that only a limited supply of goods suitable for workers to consume existed at any point in time and their real wage in terms of these goods was similarly determined. This long discarded notion encouraged no labor solidarity. Its imprint endures on craft union policy a century after economists discarded it. Industrial unionists tended instead to reckon that the gains of workers anywhere enlarge the market and the bargaining opportunities for other workers and also raise the standard against which their wages tend to be compared. The conflict between the two types of unionism was more than a struggle between union officers to retain their posts and powers. It ran through the racial prejudices of the rank and file and the deceptive hope of winning a bit of security by limiting the number who could compete for one's job. The industrial union view had its advocates within the trade unions too, their views regularly expressed and repressed at AFL conventions.

As industry modernized the older craft view became increasingly inappropriate. In 1892 the Homestead steel strike confirmed this (8) but the pivotal conflict between the two union outlooks came on the railroads in the mid-nineties. Eugene Debs of the Locomotive Firemen (24) had seen one craft union after another strike against a railroad only to have its strike broken by the other crafts that remained at work. He launched the American Railway Union for all workers in the railroad industry and with it 9,000 Great Northern men in April 1894 won a victory in the teeth of the depression. The United States Strike Commission described the new union thus:-

"The theory underlying this movement is that the organization of different classes of railroad employees upon the trade union idea has ceased to be useful or adequate; that pride of organization, petty jealousies and the conflict of views into which men are trained in separate organizations under different leaders, tend to defeat the common object of all and enable the railroads to use such organizations against each other. . .; that the rapid concentration of capital and management demands a like union of their employees; that the interests of each of the 850,000 railroad employees of the United States as to wages, treatment, hours of labor, legislation, insurance, mutual aid are common to all, and hence all ought to belong to one organization that will assert its united strength in the protection of the right of every member." (59)

The pay of the men and women who built the Pullman Palace Sleeping cars in Pullman's company town out of Chicago was cut in that 1893 depression so that many took home only statements of what they still owed the company. They struck, and when George Pullman refused to talk with them, the new ARU felt obliged to refuse to haul any Pullman cars until he did (12). Confronted by injunctions, federal troops and old guard craft unionists, the ARU was routed in June (8). It was a defeat that for years cast the American labor movement in the image of Gompers instead of the dream of Debs. Two months before it, on April 21 the UMW had ventured to make its first call for a nationwide coal strike, and though 125,000 came out, most went back beaten. In Alabama where the miners also demanded an end to convict labor in the mines, the two strikes merged into a labor revolt promptly put down by the state militia (57).

In these years Mother Jones developed an interest in the socialist hope of going beyond the trade union aim of restricting the exploitation of labor to that of completely ending that exploitation through the social ownership and democratic control of the means of production. The paper *The Appeal to Reason* started publication August 30, 1895 and this dates some of the events she gives in Chapter IV. In March 1896 she was in the Birmingham area for the *Appeal* and had the help of miners and railroad workers to enable Debs to speak at the forbidden meeting she describes on page 116 (37-A). Debs was touring the area to speak to the ARU lodges there for the last time, for on June 15, 1897 Debs and the remaining members of the ARU dissolved that industrial union for railroad workers and instead established a new effort, the Social Democracy of America, with Mother Jones attending its birth (21:76).

On July 4, 1897 the UMW, though down to 9,000 members, ventured a new nationwide strike call. Response was good. In the Central Competitive Field (western Pennsylvania, Ohio, Indiana and Illinois) the union fought off a 20 per cent cut, won a gain in the Pittsburgh district and established the bargaining procedure for the Central Competitive Field that won it the 8-hour day April 1, 1898, the checkoff of union dues in 1899, and raised the national membership to 115,000 by 1900 (42:21). Though the 1897 strike was defeated in West Virginia it raised the membership there from 200 to 3600. The anthracite fields that lie in sections of eastern Pennsylvania had not been called out, but on September 10 as the bituminous strike was being settled, the sheriff's forces killed 28 miners and wounded a score more at Lattimer in a strike called by unorganized immigrant mule drivers (1:201). They had quit work when they were told to work two extra hours without pay because the barns for several mines had been consolidated. It once more started these hard coal miners organizing.

Mother Jones was thoroughly involved in this 1897 strike. With Gompers and Debs, and Sovereign of the Knights and other labor leaders she attended a meeting at Wheeling on July 27 to assure the West Virginia miners of wide labor backing, but her main work was in the Pittsburgh area. Lois McLean quotes from the old Amalgamated Steel and Iron Workers paper the *National Labor Tribune* of August 26, 1897:

> "The woman we wish to speak of is Mrs. Mary Jones of Chicago. She has done more missionary work for the miners in the Pittsburgh district than any two officials and done it better. To her, more than to anyone else, the miners owe much of their success in this unpleasantness. She has roughed it in this district for four weeks in all kinds of weather".

xi

She organized the wives of the miners of that district, marched their children to gain more friendly publicity and led parades of farmers bringing wagons of food to the miners' Camp Determination in that strike to end the 12-hour day (37). Here she was spoken of as "Mrs. Mary Jones of Chicago". In Omaha where she had sold the *Appeal* the *Bee* referred to her participation in the Wheeling meeting of July 27 as "Mrs. Mary E. Jones known to us as a friend of labor". The year before when she arranged that Debs could speak in Birmingham she was "Mrs. Mary Jones of Kansas" connected with the *Appeal.* But by 1900 when Kerr launched the *International Socialist Review* it advertised in the *United Mine Workers' Journal* that "Mother Jones" would write in it, and she signed her first article there (March 1901) as "Mother Jones". It dealt with her observations on child labor in the deep south. Following the 1897 strike she spoke in Nashville on Labor Day and again October 1, meanwhile visiting the socialist colony at Ruskin, Tenn. (J:28 and 37-A). She attended the Social Democracy second convention in summer of 1898.

In May 1899 the miners at Arnot, Pa., asked the Erie Company for an increase such as had been given in other areas. In July they struck a thousand strong but by the end of September were ready to go back defeated (J:31). Mother Jones arrived October 1, renewed their spirits, got farmers to help feed their children and Blossburg families to house the evicted. Marcus (35) indicates Populist sentiment in this region north and west of the anthracite fields had helped turn defeat into a partial victory. That same year the UMW got a good foothold in Kansas, Arkansas and Indian Territory (later called Oklahoma) but not in Colorado.

Through 1900 Mother Jones drew $494.81 from the UMW (40) for work mostly in the two great unorganized fields that most menaced its contracts elsewhere: West Virginia whose rich and cheaply mined hills were taking over ever more of the bituminous market, and the hard coal fields of Pennsylvania owned by a handful of banks and railroads with a traditionally separate market, but still coal. On April 11, the UMW called out all District 11 in Maryland, the so-called riot at Lonaconing (J:89) occurring June 22, (29:313) with Mother Jones present.

She was then assigned to the New River territory around Montgomery in West Virginia (44:Ch. III). The New River joins the Gauley River at Gauley Bridge upstream from Montgomery and then becomes known as the Kanawha which is fed by such historic waters as Paint and Cabin Creeks from the hills to its south and by the Elk River from the north, past the capitol at Charleston to join the Ohio. In September she headed for new adventures in anthracite country.

Of the 142,500 anthracite miners the UMW at this time had less than 8,000, but it called on all hard coal miners to quit work on September 17. In the days preceding the strike Mother Jones held meetings in Mahoney City, Locust Gap, Shamokin and other towns (J-89). In the back country the walkout on the 17th was incomplete, partly from fear, partly from a disbelief that the miners would walk out in other valleys. "In the early morning hours of September 23 an army of women led by Mother Jones marched to Coleraine and Beaver Meadows and as a result the miners at Coleraine returned to their homes" (44). On September 25 (J:90 & 21:41) she made her memorable march to Coaldale in Panther Creek. Her 1915 testimony (54:10620) adds these details to the account she gives in Chapter XII:

"There were 5,000 men there that had to be got out. . . I gathered up 2,000 or 3,000 women and naturally the men followed. . . I had to go into the saloons and tell them to close up. Then we marched 15 miles over the mountains from Hazleton to Panther Creek". (Her book says they marched from McAdoo, south of Hazleton some ten miles and this is probably correct.) "We met the militia in the middle of the night. . . said they would charge us with bayonets. . . It took us three hours to go back two miles. . . . I brought out the 5,000 men. We held up the street cars. . . Once in a while when a boss wanted to jump over us we picked him up and threw him over the fence to his wife and told her to take care of him. . . That thing continued until ten o'clock in the morning. . . The women had nothing but brooms and mops and they were hungry and the militia had ordered breakfast at some hotel and I told the women to go in and eat their breakfast and let the state pay for it. . So they did".

On October 7 she marched as described in Chapter XI to Lattimer, the company town where three years earlier 28 miners had been killed by the sheriff. Her 1915 testimony adds some interesting details:

"I got about 1500 women lined up, and we walked into Lattimer. It was dark, and we knocked on every door, and told them there was no work to do. . . The drivers came along to take the mules to the mines, and I had all the women centered in front of the company's store, and we had 3,000 men down at the mines that the company or sheriff knew nothing about — they had come in on different roads, and I said when he ordered the boys to take the mules to the drivers, that the mules would not scab. I kept entertaining the sheriff and general manager and deputies, and the mules came back directly without the drivers. Of course we cheered the mules. We closed those mines in the anthracite and that really was the key to the situation. They had shot 23 men in the back just three years before. I served notice on the sheriff that no 23 workers would be shot that day; that he had just as well make up his mind those mines were going to be closed, and we had no pistols or guns, nothing but just our hands". (54:10621)

Lattimer is some fifteen miles north of Hazleton and Coaldale about the same distance south of Hazleton. The women had marched before Mother Jones came to this area. Greene (27:144) tells how Big Mary Septak had led them in this area earlier. Mother Jones did add such tactical maneuvers as marching with women noisily on Lattimer to divert attention from Panther Creek recruits entering the mines before daybreak by other roads. Soon Mitchell ordered the marches stopped because of public criticism of them, though roughing up a few miners in Lattimer had prevented the serious violence that would likely have occurred otherwise. The only death that came out of a march was near Oneida where Mother Jones was not present (21:42).

In October the anthracite coal was all gone and Mark Hanna feared the strike might put Bryan into the White

House. Companies posted notices of a 10 percent increase. The miners wanted assurance it would last past election, so stayed away until new notices assured that this rate would last until next April, with pay twice a month (48:72). There was no formal settlement, no union recognition, but the miners now knew the strength that comes from acting together and the UMWA membership in the anthracite field jumped from 8,000 to 100,000. This left a third of them still outside, including some whom Mother Jones had been most proud to bring into the strike. "Lower Lehigh worked on. The area below Hazleton in Panther Creek had always been isolated and never organized." (27:165). As Mother Jones said of another situation, "Taking men into the union is just the kindergarten of their education and every force is against their further education" (J:48).

In March 1901 these terms were renewed with similar informality for one more year, and then for an extra month to May 1, 1902. Mother Jones spent a good part of 1901 in Pennsylvania at Mitchell's request and also at his request spoke up for him at the 1901 Convention (40). "In 1901 the anthracite miners out of their meager earnings made a collection to build a home for John Mitchell" writes Elsie Gluck (25:86) but he refused and said the money should be used to build a monument to those killed at Lattimer. He was then getting $1200 a year, and the average anthracite miner $377. This was the occasion for Mother Jones to admonish the miners not to buy a house for Mrs. Mitchell until they had first bought homes for their own wives (J:88). This was not the source of friction between the two; it came rather from her concern especially in 1902 to create the economic pressure of a coal shortage, and his concern to cultivate a favorable press and friends in high places.

She worked also for the miners' daughters who worked 12-hour shifts in textile mills in the area for less than 7 cents an hour (48:68) Max Hayes reported in *International Socialist Review*, Vol. I page 816, "The silk weavers' strike in Scranton which was directed by Mother Jones was won by the workers while the strike at Patterson, N. J. was lost. . . Mother besides organizing the unions is now putting in spare time in forming a union of domestic servants". She celebrated her birthday with these silk weavers during their 1901 strike and said she was 59 (37-A). In December 1901 a short strike at the Dietz mines, Norton, Virginia, resulted in the experience she tells in Chapter III (37-A). To read her eastern coal experiences in their chronological order, one should read chapter 5, then 12, then 11, then 3, then 6 through 9.

On May 12, 1902 the anthracite miners walked out again and to win had to stay out until October 23. On June 7 the West Virginia miners walked out in the Kanawha, New River, Norfolk and Western districts. Mother Jones hoped the union would put enough men and money into West Virginia to bring it into the union, and that if need be, the union would call a strike of all coal miners, to create such a coal shortage that bankers and railroads and all the powers would see to it that a union settlement was made. As a warning to operators, the UMW National Executive Board was authorized "to call sectional or national suspensions of bituminous miners in case any soft coal was shipped to anthracite markets" (25:95). The miners in Michigan, West Virginia and the three hard coal districts called for a special convention hoping to bring about this complete shutdown. Mitchell opposed it, arguing sanctity of contracts, and postponed the call for this mandatory special convention for seven weeks, "until a mine-by-mine campaign which Hanna financed had collected enough votes to defeat the sympathy strike." (62:229)

For the first week of the West Virginia strike Mother Jones was active in the Fairmont field (J:40 to J:44). A federal injunction checked her usefulness and she moved over to Clarksburg (J:44 to J:49) where she was arrested June 20 as she spoke in a field the union had rented. This she said was the first arrest in her life (47 and 54:10622). She was taken 84 miles to Parkersburg, released on bond and thus enabled to attend the special convention in Indianapolis. There Mitchell won a slight majority for his proposal: soft coal miners to keep on working and contribute a dollar a week to the strike fund; all officers getting over $60 a month to donate a quarter of their pay, and raise enough money otherwise so the miners' families

xvi

could eat no matter how long the strike lasted. This program limited organizing activities in West Virginia. So, defeated, Mother Jones returned to face Judge Jackson (J:51) on July 24. She was released and went up into the anthracite country.

There a solid strike assured a dwindling supply of hard coal. When it got dangerously low, Morgan and the Erie owners became agreeable to the arbitration proposal the union had made at the start of the strike. The public image of these moguls had been made ridiculous in late summer by the divine right claim of their spokesman George F. Baer in a letter that became widely quoted. (On page 61 Mother Jones erroneously puts it instead into the context of the 1903 arbitration hearing.) When the coal shortage really hurt and the miners were in a position to force substantial gains, with no legal or moral obligation to accept the arbitration they had proposed 160 hungry days earlier in the first week of the strike, Mitchell insisted they grasp the Roosevelt offer. The unnamed financier who invited Mother Jones to New York (J:57) may have been Nathan Strauss if one can believe that part of Michelson's story (39). Socialist comment at the time on the consequences viewed it as grasping defeat out of victory (ISR III, 436 & 616). In this connection Mother Jones notes (J:60) that Mitchell died a rich man; in 1919 he left an estate of $347,151; Elsie Gluck attributes this to the $10,000 a year the NCF paid him until the 1911 convention made him drop it or the union, and to stock market operations on his savings (25:Ch XII). The arbitration hearings did publicize anthracite conditions, as the case of Andy Chippie, 12 years old, who worked in a mine and earned 40 cents a day, but had to give all of it back to the company to apply on the debt to the company that his father had left when he had been killed four years earlier in a mine accident.

In the fall of 1902 Mother Jones returned to West Virginia where the strike dragged on to July of 1903. It won agreements there only in the Kanawha district, including the Paint and Cabin Creek valleys that run roughly parallel into the Kanawha some seven miles apart about twenty miles upstream from Charleston. This was to be her battle ground ten years later. In the intervening years the union lost Cabin Creek in a ten day strike in 1904 that some said had been instigated by Ohio operators. From 1904 on the Cabin Creek miners worked under company guards and were allowed no visitors except those approved by the company. Across the ridge Paint Creek stayed union.

In the Central Competitive Field in February 1903 the miners won a ten per cent increase without a strike and this gain extended to other areas. In the spring of 1904 operators plead poor business conditions and asked for a 5 1/2 per cent cut. Mitchell urged acceptance and union militants went along with it on the condition that all contracts, in hard or soft coal, should expire on the same date, April 1, 1906.

In the spring of 1903 Mother Jones again battled child labor. Instead of making life better the growth of factories between 1870 and 1900 had enslaved a million more children in the textile mills of the south (46). When reformers sought to curb this with state legislation they were told industry would move to other states, so they sought federal legislation. To win Theodore Roosevelt's approval for such a law was the main purpose of the march of the mill children (J:Chapter X). No such federal legislation was introduced until 1907, and not passed until 1916. It was declared unconstitutional in 1918, as was the new 1919 law in 1922. A 1924 amendment to enable Congress to legislate on child labor failed to win approval of the necessary 36 states. A law did get passed in 1938 and was declared constitutional in 1941 (11).

On May 26, 1903 the Central Textile Workers' Union had called a hundred thousand workers on strike against six hundred firms in the Philadelphia metropolitan area. Of these strikers at least 16,000 were under 16, most of them young girls. They were working 60 hours a week for wages ranging from $2 to $13. Their chief demand was to cut this work week to 55 hours. They offered to accept a cut in pay to gain this taste of freedom. Helen Camp (11) attributes the rigid refusal to concede this demand to the pressure of the intense 1903 anti-union crusade of the National Association of Manufacturers; her day by day account provides most the data for these notes.

The Children's Crusade set out July 7. It ended August 4. The strike committee had let no word of the idea slip out. At the strikers' morning mass meeting on the 7th the plan

xviii

was announced and a hundred child strikers got parental permission to join the march. It set off with an escort of some two hundred adults, with tents and provisions on a wagon, and the girls riding at noon on the Bristol Pike toward the first stop at Torresdale Park, all headed by a small boy whose placard read "We are Textile Workers". At the Park most of the army was sent back home as funds were low and the temperature in the 90's.

The next stop was Bristol, a textile center, where local authorities feared the marchers might call a strike. Next was Morrisville across from Trenton; there the 52 marchers had to pay $1.04 toll. Reception was poor at Princeton, but they had heart-warming meetings in New Brunswick and spent Saturday night across the Raritan at Highland Park, and stayed there Sunday to fight the rain and the New Jersey mosquitos. At Elizabeth they had a two day stop with a union banquet on the second day, then a poor reception at Paterson. The second Sunday was festive at the New York Social Democratic Party's annual picnic in Westchester Park, then a nights stop at Passaic and another at West Hoboken. At all stops they held meetings that often raised some two hundred dollars for the strike committee plus sustenance and accomodation for the marchers. Some left the march and went back home, and were replaced, so the size of the army varied. At West Hoboken it numbered 50. Mother Jones stayed there at a hotel and found that two Secret Service men were taking turns keeping an eye on the keyhole. The last campfire was Wednesday night at Jersey City Heights. Her troops entered New York via Christopher Street Ferry and marched with banners to the Social Democratic hall at 64 East 4th. For the evening march thence to a block from Madison Gardens, the 60 strikers were accompanied by 600 police. Though she had only three small boys with her that night, she had 40 to put in the cages at Coney Island. Sunday she sent all home except the committee, the band, the women and the three boys whom she wanted to take to the President.

Monday morning she shook the Coney Island sand off the boys and walked them to the Oriental Hotel at Manhattan Beach where she hoped to corner Senator Platt and enlist his aid to introduce a bill limiting child labor. Bostock who had entertained them at Coney Island loaned them an elephant for this walk, with GOP painted in red on its fore-head. In her 1915 testimony (54:10642) Mother Jones explained that a section hand showed them how to get past the blockade that faced them at the hotel and into the saloon. There the barkeep arranged a dramatic entrance into the dining room where the Senator sat at breakfast. But he jumped up, went out the side door and into a waiting interurban trolley. However the elephant sat down on the track and delayed its departure. The crusaders were now at breakfast, for the cook had been a miner, and missed their chance to corner the Senator. Two days later with two men and the three boys Mother Jones arrived at Oyster Bay and was denied an audience with the President by Secretary Barnes. On August 4 they returned by trolley to the city to await a reply from the president. Despite the funds they raised the strike was lost. But child labor was made into a live subject for journalists; in Pennsylvania by 1905 the law was changed to require some other proof that a child was 13 than his parents signature to an affidavit. (11)

Union coal miners had established their own cemetery at Mt. Olive, Illinois (33) when others refused to let them bury their fellow workers killed in a battle with scabs at Virden, October 12, 1898 (42:329). Mother Jones was buried there in 1930. In the fall of 1903 she had gone there to speak at a memorial service (J:95) after visiting Debs in Terre Haute. Then the Executive Board sent her to southern Colorado to check the situation there. Through the southwest since 1900 the UMW had built some organization in Missouri, Kansas, Arkansas and Indian Territory. Southern Colorado was the territory mainly of two large companies, Rockefeller's Colorado Fuel and Iron, and Victor Fuel. A 1900 organizing effort there had been wiped out. But in the north where smaller operators served a more varied public, a few had responded to the UMW invitation to meet in conference. Overshadowing the coal mine dispute was a Western Federation of Miners strike in the state's lucrative metal mines (42:334; 22:398; 49; 31:Ch. X; 30; 20:pages 5—80). This battling union had merged various metal mine unions together in 1893; it had been briefly but unhappily affiliated with the AFL, and in 1898 had launched the Western Labor Union to build general working class solidarity in its area, renaming this the American

Labor Union in 1902 and looking east. In its early days it had accepted coal miners also, but when the UMW started organizing in the west, as Haywood explained to the 1915 Commission (54:10595) it transferred them to their own industrial union.

Mother Jones made her needle-peddling check on conditions (J:95) and as she put it in her 1915 testimony, "I reported in Indianapolis that the fever was there and at fever heat. The men were wild to come out". The Colorado State Commissioner of Labor had also gone to Indianapolis to urge that no coal strike be called in Colorado. With no such promise from the union he wired back to the Governor that there would be no strike and Gluck concludes that this obliged the National Board to call one, November 9. Mother Jones recalled how the Governor was so concerned lest concurrent strikes force him to move some of his armed thugs from the metal mines to coal mines (54:10624). Similar considerations led to her clash with Mitchell who wanted to end the strike in the mines north of Denver for a 15 per cent boost twelve days after the strike had begun (J:98). She postponed that for nine days, and when the northern miners went back the southern companies started evicting strikers (25:171). The rulers of Colorado were at war with its miners, whether they dug ore or coal, a war that Governor Peabody called "a state of insurrection and rebellion". Suggs (49) shows it as part of the NAM drive to eradicate unions. Troops were hired with $776,000 borrowed from the mining companies, directed by the mining companies to do their thuggery but eventually to be repaid from taxes. They denied the right of habeas corpus or of the civil courts to interfere in their violence (31:152). A story went that a lawyer with a writ of habeas corpus for a striker held by the militia was told by General Bell, "Hell, we don't have habeas corpus here; we just have post mortems". The incidents of Chapter XIII deal with both concurrent strikes.

In late January 1904, Mother Jones working in snow-covered tent colonies was hospitalized with pneumonia, then on March 26 grabbed for deportation (J:102) but slipped to Denver. Voluntarily she went to help with the strike in Utah where she was quarantined for smallpox (J:107) but for less than the 26 days she mentions perhaps confusing this with the duration of her 1914 stay in Walsenburg jail (J:185). She returned to Trinidad, where the coal strike dragged on; union relief funds were cut off in June, but the strike continued to October. (The 1914 date given J:111 is wrong as she was in jail on that date, and is probably meant to read 1904.) In January 1904 the public relations expert in charge of Rockefeller's dirty tricks department planted a story in a Denver scandal sheet *Polly Pry* alleging that Mother Jones had been running whorehouses in Denver and other cities for years. (36:100 & 36:135 & 21:136) This story got sent out to newspapers wherever Mother Jones gave the employing class some trouble, and into the *Congressional Record* for June 13, 1914. Mother Jones never bothered to answer it, though a check with Debs, Wayland, Powderly and others could have refuted it.

After she left Colorado in 1904, as she told the 1915 Commission: "I resigned from the miners for a while; I had other things to do". Between then and 1910 she was involved in strikes of streetcarmen, railroad workers, iron miners on the Mesabi, and in between them and alongside them, spreading socialist literature and defending the Mexican opponents of dictator Diaz. In mid-August 1904 she was in New York addressing the central labor body of that city on the fight in Colorado and selling Debs' new 44-page booklet *Unionism and Socialism: A Plea for Both* (NYT Aug. 8, 1904). She explained it took six soldiers "to get me, a woman of 65, and put me on a train to get out of the country" (21:67). That is the sort of age she gave at that time and it fits in with other data gathered by Lois McLean indicating Mother Jones was probably born in 1839, not 1830. She was given and gave the greater age while imprisoned in 1913 in West Virginia. Mrs. McLean has found Toronto Normal School records for a Maria Harris who entered it at age 18 in 1858, and left it in 1859. She believes this is the same young teacher whom Sister Raffaele discovered in this passage in Sister Rosalita's book *No Greater Service: The History of the Congregation of the Sisters, Servants of the Immaculate Heart of Mary:-* "The old memorandum under date of August 31, 1859 reads: 'Miss M. Harris entered the house as a secular teacher'. She remained until March 8, 1860 at which time she was paid in full $36.43".

"The other things to do" that Mother Jones had in mind in 1904 probably included work for railroad shopmen who were being denied the right to bargain collectively instead of by crafts, (J:114). In 1902 the shop crafts on Union Pacific and Santa Fe had decided on that policy, and the brotherhoods that move the trains hauled rolling stock that needed repairs to Southern Pacific shops in California, so the strike extended there. From 1904 to 1908 some of her old friends in the deep south on the Louisville and Nashville had the same trouble for several years and she helped them. It was the ARU industrial union issue all over again. So in January 1905 when her Western Federation friends asked her to join with them in sponsoring a new labor movement to reorganize all American labor along industrial lines she signed their Manifesto, and attended the June 1905 congress in Chicago, which declared itself the Industrial Workers of the World. John Walker and others from the United Mine Workers were there too, rather to look and see than to commit their union to join, for they wanted such a structure as the IWW was building but felt like Brewery Workers and others who shared their hopes that it would have to be large to provide them with the backing they needed. When the convention ended with little more support than its January sponsors they stayed away (52:21). No mention of this venture is made in her book. She did a year later speak on behalf of Western Federation leaders when they were framed on a murder charge (Chapter XV and 48), aid in its forlorn 1907 Mesaba Range strike and its 1913 Michigan copper strike, but this was aid to the Western Federation not the new revolutionary union from which it soon departed too; she did protest the Bisbee deportation (J:176) which involved members of both the WFM and IWW, and in 1921 work for a resolution for release of all class war prisoners, mostly IWW's, at the Pan-American Labor congress; the AFL did use her to bring IWW strikers under its influence as in May, 1916 at the McCormick binder twine plant in Chicago, something she was able to do only because she shared so much of their hope and spirit. It is notable that her book excludes mention of her part in the launching of the IWW, and her efforts to free Tom Mooney (23), two issues on which her friends in the labor movement were much divided.

In January 1906 UMW met looking ahead to expiration of all its contracts April 1. It aimed at inclusion of the southwest into the bituminous conference with operators in central field too, an 8 hour day, a 12 1/2 per cent boost and no one under 16 to work in the mines. The operators met the southwest proposal with the taunt why hadn't the union organized West Virginia. In February a special convention resolved that "no contract be signed until we all get a settlement or go down in defeat together" (25:185) but soon it was decided to work where operators restored the 1903 cut, leaving other miners on strike for a long, long time. The Colorado strikes of 1903-1904 had been lost, forcing the more active UMW and WFM to leave the state. John Lawson tried again in the south with no success, but in the north in 1907 he obtained contracts with 17 companies to run to 1910. The big southern companies pressed these operators in 1910 not to renew them, and Mother Jones' warning of November 1903 (J:99 and 21:62) became reality. The UMW again called her to Colorado. Her 1915 testimony (54:10627) described her chief activity as getting 15 miners out of jail. President White of the UMW induced her to propose that this UMW strike be called off. She did make this proposal, and when it proved unpopular, she became the scapegoat (21:112 and 5). It was made out that her proposal aimed to befriend her radical friends in the WFM, but they had already lost out in that union to more conservative officers who by this time were arranging to bring WFM back into the AFL (31:242). The UMW sent her instead to Westmoreland County in Pennsylvania where the women sang themselves out of jail (J:Ch XVII & 54:10627). At the 1911 UMW convention she again urged a strike in southern Colorado to win that field and help the miners north of Denver.

In 1910 also she found time to help women bottlers on strike against Milwaukee breweries and shirtwaist makers in New York (40). She was soon back with the railroad shop crafts who struck the entire Harriman system Sept. 30, 1911 to late 1915 to demand their right to bargain collectively instead of craft by craft. She was speaking on their behalf in Butte in June 1912 when she heard that her

Paint Creek miners in West Virginia were locked in battle again.

That spring the UMW had negotiated a 5 per cent increase on tonnage rates effective April 1 (7). Of the 69,600 miners in West Virginia only 1136 were in the union. By May first they had had to give up the check-off to get a similar boost. Then Quinn Morton argued that his agreement covering his Paint Creek Colleries ran to 1914, left the conference, hired Baldwin Felts guards, borrowed some machine guns and posted notices the miners must work under the old terms or vacate their homes. It started as a strike confined to 14 mines in Paint Creek but at issue was whether the state now producing 70 million tons of coal a year was to become union. It developed into a major industrial war.

The evicted miners set up a tent colony at Holly Grove near the mouth of Paint Creek. Five miles away the Baldwin Felts set up camp by a major colliery at Mucklow. After the first armed battle between the two, June 5, a grand jury indicted the guards for killing a miner, but through the whole bloody war no guard ever served a day in jail. The main strike demand was get rid of the guards. There were 2,500 Baldwin Felts guards alone in the state and some from other agencies (60). West across the ridge in Cabin Creek the miners had lived for 8 years with guards deciding · who could come in to see them. (On page 149 the names of these two creeks are reversed.) Many had been lured in by lies and kept there by force and terror. The Paint Creek men were fighting against being reduced to this position. In the "third Battle of Mucklow" July 26, strikers were stopped from silencing the machine guns, when the guards marched scores of arrested strikers to stand in front as hostages (38).

The UMWA had no other big struggle at the time and there was hope that now the state would be brought into the union. When miners from Cabin Creek asked for an organizer (41:27) Mother Jones headed for Eskdale, the one townsite along the creek where she would not be on company property. There on August 6 she held the first union meeting in many years (J:158). On the 13th Fred Mooney watched Mother Jones bluff the mine guards with her hand over the machine gun (J:156, 41:28, 21:89).

West, the Baltimore reporter who accompanied her walk in the icy creek to Wineburg (J:159) wrote of that in his illustrated article in Survey (60). On August 15 she and others spoke from the statehouse steps in Charleston, some three thousand miners joining in the demonstration to abolish the guard system. Mikeal appends a verbatim report of this speech; it does not urge anyone to buy guns, but her book (J:171) and her testimony (54:10629) emphasize such advice. She had more than this one meeting in Charleston. By August one merchant there had sold over a thousand rifles (7). On September 1 miners tried to cross the Kanawha and drive the scabs and guards out of both creeks, but were stopped by superior firepower. On the second the Governor declared the first of three periods of martial law, this one lasting to Oct. 15. The militia at first disarmed miners and guards alike and were welcomed for a time by the miners. From the guards 10,000 dumdum bullets were taken, forbidden by the laws of war (38). As martial law ended many militia members went into company guard service without even changing their uniforms, the companies replaced the weaponry taken from the guards and the miners were left unarmed and vulnerable (38:616). After a new declaration of martial law on Nov. 15, Mother Jones toured major cities urging a Congressional investigation of the strike. Martial law ended January 10, with the militia once more going back to company hire, and on February 7, 1913 came the attack from the armed C&O train called the Bullmoose Special on the helpless women and children at Holly Grove (J:161 & 21:95). The miners again attacked Mucklow and Governor Glasscock renewed martial law. Mother Jones and a committee of 35 came to see the Governor, were arrested by special constables in the sight of open civil courts, taken by train into the strike zone where martial law applied, where one Charleston reporter got arrested after seeing her and 98 other all tried by a military tribunal in three days (7). On February 20 a petition was filed with the state supreme Court of Appeals to bring these prisoners before a civil court; a month later the court OK'd the military tribunal and its actions. Meanwhile on March 4 Governor Hatfield had replaced Governor Glasscock. He visited Mother Jones, found her ill with pneumonia, had her taken to a Charleston physician, then returned to "house arrest" in Pratt. He released some of her associates but kept her. On May 14 she sent her telegram to Sen. Kern (J:165). That and widespread concern over her health and imprisonment led Hatfield to release her. On May 16 she listened to Senate discussion of Kern's resolution, travelled to urge public pressure on its behalf and it was passed May 27. Mother Jones attended the sessions of the resultant investigating committee June 10 to 18 with an unusual silence, perhaps influenced by important events in the two creeks going on at the same time, and to avoid a crossfire.

Hatfield had arranged a May 1 settlement that cost the operators little: no union recognition, no change in rates, no ending of the mine guard system, only the 9-hour day, semi-monthly pay with right to have a checkweighman (17). *The Huntington Socialist and Labor Star* which had been bootlegged into the strike zone during the strike pointed out that the miners in Paint and Cabin Creek were in a position to demand and get more. Its printshop was raided and wrecked on the personal orders of Governor Hatfield (17:23). The National Executive Committee of the Socialist Party sent an investigating committee consisting of Debs, Berger and Germer, instructing it to work in harmony with the UMW officials who had recommended accepting the Hatfield terms. The Socialist committee "exonerated" Hatfield on June 4, by getting Debs confused about dates and other data. But while the Senate committee was still investigating, the Paint and Cabin Creek miners walked out again on June 15 and in a very short strike won union recognition, end of mine guard rule, an 8-hour day and the Kanawha scale (17:15). This laid the basis for successful union missionary work through the state except its southern edge (21:103 and ref. 13 chap. 11).

After helping in the 1913 Michigan copper strike (21:141 & 31:Ch 16) Mother Jones headed for Texas for a Labor Day speech, then to Trinidad to build attendance at the Sept. 15 UMWA convention that she hoped would either get union recognition in this southern field that produced 60 per cent of the state's coal, or strike it. On September 23 two thousand struck in the north and nine thousand in the south, the latter living in company houses so the union at once set up tent colonies (36:110). The operators brought in Baldwin-Felts thugs and the same machine guns Mother Jones had faced a few months earlier in West Virginia. They made their first attack on the main Ludlow tent colony on October 7 but killing none until Colorado Fuel and Iron set up a 5000 candle power searchlight to vex the colony. On October 21 Mother Jones organized a woman's demonstration in front of the hotel where Governor Ammon visited the strike zone; after he left three strikers were shot at Walsenburg. UMW offered a settlement not involving recognition but were turned down. The state auditor Kenehan was a member of the Blacksmiths and gave the strikers some hope by refusing approval of the $4,000 a day the militia cost. However the companies took care of these costs until the state supreme court ordered Kenehan to pay. Mother Jones, ill, went to Washington in November to urge investigation. December 3 the worst blizzard in 30 years hit the tent colonies. On the 16th the State Federation of Labor held a convention and staged the protest parade, photo facing page 202. (That Christmas the nation heard of the tragedy at Calumet, Michigan where the strikers Mother Jones had been helping held a Christmas party for their children in a second story hall; some fiend hollered 'Fire' and in the stampede down the stairway 72, mostly children, were crushed to death (31:285).

From Denver Mother Jones had gone to El Paso (J:187) and came back to Trinidad on January 4, on the 8 a.m. train. A bit over an hour later the militia had her on a train bound for Denver. Chase said that if she returned he would jail her incommunicado (36:171). She did return on January 11 (J:179) and was put into the Mount San Rafael Hospital on the outskirts of the city and kept there under armed guard for nine weeks (J:183) being released March 15 to avoid a state supreme court hearing on her bid for habeas corpus scheduled for the following day. Meanwhile atrocities had multiplied. On January 21 Gen. Chase fell off his horse while trying to break up a women's demonstration on behalf of Mother Jones, then ordered his troops to ride the women down and many were injured. This enabled Senator Keating of Colorado to get his resolution for an investigation of the strike out of the Rules Committee and passed. Its hearing began February 9. Gen. Chase refused to be questioned by it. On March 10 the troops tore down the tent colony at Forbes exposing the women and children to severe weather (36:187). After six days' freedom Mother Jones entrained for Trinidad again March 21, but was taken off at Walsenburg and locked up in the rat-infested basement of the courthouse (J:185 & 36:191). She was released on April 17 and went to Washington to urge intervention, her testimony on this being reported NYT April 24. Meanwhile on April 19, the Easter Sunday of the Orthodox Church to which many southern miners belonged, came the gruesome attack on the Ludlow tent colony (J:192). McGovern, who devotes chapter 14 to the most detailed account of this atrocity, destroys all ground for considering it an accident. Major Hamrock had been at Wounded Knee and Lieut. Linderfelt **had previous training in sadism in suppressing a** Phillipine insurrection. By the time they were through, in the cellar under the Pandragon family tent the bodies of fifteen were found burned to death. Strikers poured in with whatever guns they could find to chase the scabs out, giving them free exit if they turned in their arms. On April 30 federal troops took over. The pious Rockefeller refused any arbitration lest it result in unionization (36:257). The strike was ended with a settlement in September 1914 that gave them nothing. No company hirelings were indicted, but 408 UMW men were charged with various offenses, some, including John Lawson, with murder. In July of 1915 Lawson was convicted in a company dominated court. Mother Jones traveled speaking for his defense, and he was saved to become an officer of Victor Fuel in 1917 when it made a brief contract with the union. In 1914 and 1915 she traveled extensively speaking for the most part on the Colorado strike, at Cooper Union on May 22, 1914 and then to suffragettes providing the occasion for the photo facing page 203.

On Jan. 15, 1915, Mother Jones was in Washington to hear Rockefeller Jr. testify before the Industrial Relations Commission. With some UMW officers she visited him at 26 Wall Street on the 27th, but it did no good. On Jan. 21, 1915 she was at Roosevelt, N.J. (J:236 and 21:142). She gave two remarkable days of testimony to the Industrial Relations Commission, May 13 and 14, running to some 20,000 indignant words (54).

In the fall of 1915 she helped the Western Federation

in the Arizona strike (31:366) which she misdates as 1913 (J:172). The old WFM was now the International Union of Mine Mill & Smelter Workers, an AFL affiliate. George W.P. Hunt had been elected governor of the new state in 1911, safely re-elected in 1914, counted out in the close 1916 race, but by a recount restored to office. Though she was outraged by the Bisbee deportation (J:176, but more fully described in 42:399, or 50 or 20:385 or 35) the IWW was mediated out of the Arizona picture by her labor friends. The 1916 frame-up of Tom Mooney (23) gave her another cause to defend for the rest of her life. In the fall of that year she was accused of urging the wives of striking New York transit workers to acts of violence (21:147). She was also active in the Indiana elections to the dismay of her socialist friends supporting the Democratic ticket on which her friend Senator Kern was running for re-election, rather than the Socialist ticket on which Debs was running for Congress. Kern and Debs both lost (21:153).

In 1917 she was with her friend Fred Mooney in various parts of West Virginia again (21: 148 & 21:178) and again there in 1919 to protest prison conditions (J: Ch. 23). With amazing vitality for her age she threw herself into preparations for the 1919 steel strike (J: Ch24) speaking to large crowds at Pittsburgh August 12, and at Homestead on August 20, where she had to help the jailer get the crowds outside the jail to head home. The strike did not start until September 22. It was killed by the old prejudices and phoney patriotic appeals that she had long been fighting, while the loose alliance of craft unions was no match for the industrial power structure and terrorism it faced (8). It was time for the coal miners to enforce long postponed wage demands with a strike threat that would have taken some pressure off the steel workers too, but on November 10 John L. Lewis declared that the UMW could not strike when the government said not to. The steel strike collapsed. All this left its imprint on Mother Jones. Within the UMW it strengthened her sympathies for the opponents of John L. Lewis, as Howat who was fighting the compulsory arbitration law in Kansas (21:171). Outside the UMW it strengthened her friendship for steel strike leader William Z. Foster even when his 1923 pro-Communist finagling at the Farmer-Labor Party convention led to a temporary rupture with her old friend John Fitzpatrick of the Chicago Federation of Labor (J:238 and 21:197). However Fitzpatrick remained one of her closest friends to her death.

Despite increasing frailty she obviously enjoyed her 1921 trip to Mexico City to attend the Pan-American Labor Congress (J:238). Fred Mooney accompanied her and wrote an extensive description of the trip (41). She indeed had friends there. Her rescue of Manuel Sarabia back in 1907 after he had been kidnaped by connivance of American and Mexican authorities had made her a heroine to those who had rescued the land from Diaz. That kidnaping had occurred June 30, 1907 while she was speaking outdoors in Douglas to rally support for a WFM strike that had started in Arizona Territory on April 10 (31:359). Thus the still earlier contact that she mentions with opponents of Diaz at bottom of page 142 must have been before 1908; the 1901 date on page 142 should surely read 1921, and the quotation marks throughout the chapter are misleading. Prof. William G. Whittaker who presented a paper "'Mother' Mary Jones and Mexico: The Defense of the Mexican Exiles, 1907-1910" at the Northwest Labor History Conference, Seattle, 1971, believes her contact with progressive forces in Mexico may have started during the Cripple Creek strike of 1903-1904. Strikes in the southwest states have often made it very desirable to arrange with friends of unionism across the border to spread the facts of the strike and discourage the export of strikebreakers. It was for that purpose that she had gone to El Paso during the 1914 strike (J:187), and during that strike Villa had protested her imprisonment. It was for the same purpose back in 1911 after the fall of the Diaz dictatorship she had gone with Frank Hayes of the UMW and Joe Cannon of the WFM to visit Madero (J:143). The fight against Diaz had warmed the hearts of all American radicals (6). The Kerr Company had published the classic indictment of Diaz *"Barbarous Mexico"* by John Kenneth Turner who with Mother Jones was a main witness before the 1910 Rules Committee hearing that investigated the persecutions of Mexican citizens by Diaz. The Antonio Villarreal whom she had befriended earlier (J:143) was a cabinet minister in 1921 anxious to accomodate her in any way he could to tour Mexican industries (J:239 and 41). The Pan-American Labor Congress was held in January; her major achievement there was the adoption of a resolution that did not fit the designs of those who wanted to use the Congress for the glorification of the American or other governments who had political prisoners (32). Later that year she returned to Mexico briefly to vacation at a home provided by Villarreal (21:176).

During World War I, Mother Jones, Fred Mooney and other UMW organizers had continued their efforts to organize West Virginia. Her message of discontent with a 20 per cent wage increase, with spiralling cost of living and coal at $6 a ton was felt by some operators to clash unpatriotically with their wartime profit; and some UMW officers felt her line was inexpedient. After the war the operators in the Southern counties refused to deal with the union (21:180) and in Logan County paid the sheriff $2,275 a month to hire deputies to keep organizers out. In August 1919 while Mother Jones was away helping steel workers get ready to strike, union miners in Kanawha and New River districts assembled to march on Logan and Mingo Counties to make them safe for organizers. Some officials opposed this march, and those who did get to the Logan County border were turned back by the threat of federal troops and charges of treason. In August 1921 continued assault on union men led Mother Jones to urge that miners march on Logan County again and free the arrested unionists. Several thousand responded. Governor Morgan asked for federal troops and airplanes armed with machine guns to be used for the first time against American workers (21:185). Mother Jones then tried to stop the march with a telegram purportedly from President Harding that she had concocted, urging the miners to go home and promising an end to "the gunman system". This wire was at once proved phoney, but the march broke up and the men went back on trains to Charleston. Soon Logan County deputies entered union territory to arrest union men, and the fighting was renewed giving General Mitchell his chance to prove what airplanes and machine guns and tear gas could do to striking miners. The strike in these southern counties dragged on to the fall of 1922. In the spring of 1923 (J:233) Mother Jones got Governor Morgan to release a number of miners convicted for their part in this civil war.

Next year, 1924, while she was in Chicago working on her *Autobiography* the dressmakers fought and lost a five month battle in which over 1500 of them were arrested. She was there to encourage them, but this was her last direct involvement in a labor dispute. In 1929 North Carolina textile strikes she "itched to be there" (21:201). The entire twenties, well called *The Lean Years* (4), disappointed her. For the first time union membership shrunk in a business up-swing. Union-busting got named "the American Plan"; corporations milking new public relations techniques asserted a moral ascendancy; almost all militant labor struggles were made by groups left of center. William Green, former coal miner, become president of the American Federation of Labor toured the country speaking to Rotary Clubs and Chambers of Commerce promising if they would help organize their workers he would send union-paid efficiency experts to make them more profitable. She did maintain her efforts on behalf of Tom Mooney and other union men in prison and spoke up for Sacco and Vanzetti, two non-union self-employed anarchists.

On November 24, 1927 she wrote Fitzpatrick that she was now out of Garfield Hospital and added: "I will be 99 the first day of next May and I want to live to be 100 and come to Chicago to celebrate the anniversary". In May 1929 she started living with a coal-mining family, the Burgesses, who had a home near Washington at Hyattsville, Md. There on May 1, 1930 she celebrated a hundredth birthday with newsreel cameras and many dignitaries present, and exchanged birthday congratulations with the Rockefellers. On June 30 she wrote Fitzpatrick: "I was overwhelmed by the expressions of the great numbers of my friends who remembered my hundredth birthday". On November 30, 1930 she died there. Newspapers ran kindly recollections of her fight for great causes; labor leaders and politicians attended her funeral, both in Washington and Mt. Olive, Illinois. It was again a time of widespread hunger and the issue of the New York Times that records her funeral devotes its lead article to explaining that while it was constitutional for the government to provide fodder for starving cattle, it was not constitutional to provide food for starving people. It editorialized on Mother Jones: "Her special faculty was the arrangement of pageants of poverty, processions of the ill used". The new times needed a dozen more of her.

There is much not known about Mother Jones, especially not known for sure. Outside of sources mentioned in the appended bibliography, her correspondence can be found in the John Fitzpatrick papers in the Chicago Historical Society, in the Thomas Morgan and John Walker papers, University of Illinois, in Mother Jones' and John Mitchell's papers at the Catholic University in Washington, in the Adolph Germer papers at State Historical Society Madison and in the Otto Branstetter papers at Taminent Institute. A source apparently untapped so far is the manuscript by Lillie Mae Burgess who took care of Mother Jones in her final years. The Burgesses renamed their place The Mother Jones Rest Home, prospered, and in 1936 built an annex. Fetherling's and McGovern's books cite the various relevant government documents. National Archives Conciliation file 33-39 deals with her activities in West Virginia, and file 22-131 with her efforts on behalf of New York clothing workers. Her own book, errors, enigmas and all, remains the primary source.

How was the book prepared?· Why are her efforts on behalf of Mooney, Schmidt, McNamara and the IWW not mentioned? Why were easily detectable errors not corrected?

Does the book reflect some bias of the publisher, Kerr, or the editor, Mary Field Parton? This seems unlikely. Kerr then as now was a publisher of labor and socialist literature and very friendly to the IWW, Mooney and similar causes. Mrs. Parton had graduated from the University of Michigan in 1902, gone into social work in Chicago, and according to her obituary in the Chicago Tribune (7-5-69) "covered labor news for several magazines after graduation". Under her maiden name Mary G. Field she wrote such articles as "On the Witness Stand, The Workingman's Wife" in the *Delineator*, September 1910, "On Strike" in the *American Magazine* October 1911, and "Drama of Wages" in *American Magazine* November 1912. These are vivid and effective presentations of the workers' case, worthy of use in social history studies today, and her vignettes in the *Delineator* November 1911 and January

1912 whether they are reportage or fiction show that her heart beat to the same drum as Mother Jones'.

Mikeal (40:135) quotes a 1924 letter from Mother Jones in Chicago to Emma Powderly about how tired she was of writing her book. It makes no mention of Mrs. Parton. Did Mrs. Parton edit the manuscript Mother Jones wrote, or take it down as dictation? It seems no one asked Mrs. Parton about this though she lived to 91 and died only in 1969. Various errors are of the sort most likely to occur in dictation, as "Roughner Hotel" (J:162) for what Mother Jones surely knew as the Ruffner Hotel, or "Mrs. M.F. Langdon" (J:110) for her close and first-name friend Emma F. Langdon. Or did it get written from her testimony before various commissions and committees, from magazine and newspaper articles? There are close parallels to the 1915 testimony, but too many differences and discrepancies for this to seem likely. How come neither Mother Jones nor her friends nor Kerr nor Mrs. Parton seemed to have checked it for obvious errors? Mother Jones never bothered to refute misstatements whether they attacked her or made her legendary. It would be interesting to have Powderly's comment on the legend (21:10 and 44:Chapter I) that he had initiated her into the Knights shortly after the Chicago fire because of the questions she asked after his lecture— for he did not join the Knights until 1876 and women were not admitted until 1881. Powderly died in 1924, but his widow, Emma, had been his secretary and was a close friend to Mother Jones, able to correct many of its errors. Did Mother Jones ever comment on the oft-quoted one-page article by Peter C. Michelson in the *Delineator*, May 1915 that has Mother Jones born in 1833, making Mrs. Lincoln's inaugural dress in 1860, touring southern coal fields with her husband George Jones, then, after the death of George and her children in 1867, breaking her health in an investigation of southern textile mills, and so accepting a sewing position in a San Francisco household in 1877, but instead getting involved in Dennis Kearney's anti-Chinese agitation, then traveling the country as an agitator who often walked the streets at night for lack of money to go to a hotel, directing the Hocking Valley strike in 1882 and getting young William McKinley fresh out of law school to defend the miners charged with murder in that strike? The article has a fine drawing of Mother Jones but the Hocking Valley strike was in 1884 and McKinley was admitted to the bar in 1867 at age 34. Yet, misprints and all, this book remains a great piece of working class literature.

That Mother Jones also became a legend is in itself an important fact of history. Myths grow from roots in widely held wishes and dramatize them. The painful powerlessness of working people who could instead, if organized to do it, run the world for their collective benefit—this generates the mass wish that cries "Mother, come organize us" and the traditional image perhaps most vividly recorded in the recollections of folk-singer John Farrance, author of one of the versions of the ballad "The Death of Mother Jones" (26) as he wrote them for labor folklorist Archie Green:

"I saw her one time in Monongahela. She was trying to organize the mines. She came down Pike Street in a buggy and horse. Two company thugs grabbed the horse by the bridle and told her to turn around and get back down the road. She wore a gingham apron and she reached under it and pulled out a special .38 pistol and told them to turn her horse loose, and they sure did. She continued on to the park and spoke to a large crowd of miners. She wasn't afraid of the devil".

Fred Thompson
July 1974

BIBLIOGRAPHY

References to these books and articles are made in the introduction by the number assigned in this alphabetic arrangement, and page or section. "J" is used instead of a number for references to the present volume. Those deemed most helpful are so noted in some comment here.

1. Aurand, Harold W., *From the Molly Maguires to the United Mine Workers:* Philadelphia, Temple University Press 1971. Good source on early anthracite.

2. Bailey, Kenneth R., "A Judicious Mixture: Negroes and Immigrants in West Virginia Mines" in *West Virginia History* Vol. 34:141-161.

3. Bayard, Charles J., "The 1927-1928 Colorado Coal Strike" in *Pacific Historical Review* Vol. 32.

4. Bernstein, Irving, *The Lean Years,* Houghton Mifflin, 1960. Very readable and informed account of the labor movement 1920-1932.

5. Beshoar, Barron B., *Out of the Depths* Denver Trades & Labor Assembly 1942. An account of John R. Lawson.

6. Blaisdell, Lowell L., *The Desert Revolution,* University of Wisconsin Press, 1964: on fight against Diaz.

7. Blizzard, Wm. Jr., "The Battle of Paint Creek" in *The Mountain Messenger,* Peytona, W. Va., Sept. and Nov. issues 1973.

8. Brecher, Jeremy, *Strike!* Straight Arrow Books, San Francisco, 1972. A lively account of 1877, Homestead, Pullman, 1919 steel strike, etc.

9. Brooks, Thomas R., *Toil and Trouble,* Dell 1971 (Delacourt 1964) A brief history of American labor last century and this.

10. Bruce, Robert V., *1877: A Year of Violence,* Bobbs-Merrill, 1959.

11. Camp, Helen, "Mother Jones and the Children's Crusade" unpublished M.A. thesis, Columbia University 1969.

12. Carwardine, Rev. William H., *The Pullman Strike* (1894) new edition with introduction by Virgil J. Vogel, Kerr 1974.

13. Chaplin, Ralph, *Wobbly* University of Chicago Press, 1948.

14. Coleman, McAlister, *Men and Coal,* Farrar and Rinehart, 1943. Arno reprint, 1969.

15. . . . . . (with H. S. Raushenbush) *Red Neck,* a coal mine novel.

16. . . . . . *Eugene V. Debs, A Man Unafraid* Greenberg Publishers, 1930, an excellent biography, very readable.

17. Corbin, David, *The Socialist & Labor Star* Appalachian Movement Press, Huntington, W. Va., 1971 (or similar account in *West Virginia History* Vol. 34.)

18. Cornell, Robert, *The Anthracite Coal Strike of 1902,* Catholic University Press, 1957.

19. David, Henry, *The History of the Haymarket Affair* Farrar and Rhinehart, 1936 or Russel & Russel 1958; the outstanding account of this tragedy.

20. Dubofsky, Melvyn *"We Shall Be All".* Quadrangle, 1969, a history of IWW and WFM.

21. Fetherling, Dale, *Mother Jones the Miners' Angel,* Southern Illinois University Press, 1974 - the most complete account yet of Mother Jones.

22. Foner, Philip S., *History of the Labor Movement in the United States* International Publishers. Vol. III, 1947, covers AFL in Mother Jones' active years, and Vol. IV, 1965, covers IWW 1905-1915.

23. Frost, Richard H., *The Mooney Case* Stanford University Press, 1968, Outstanding study of Tom Mooney Frame-up and California power structure.

24. Ginger, Ray, *Eugene V. Debs: A Biography,* Collier 1962 reprint of *The Bending Cross,* Rutgers Unisity Press (1947).

25. Gluck, Elsie, *John Mitchell, Miner,* John Day Co., 1929.

26. Green, Archie, *Only a Miner: Studies in Recorded Coal-Mining Songs* University of Illinois Press, 1971; includes data of his "The Death of Mother Jones" in *Labor History,* Vol. 1 (1960).

27. Greene, Victor R., *The Slavic Community on Strike,* University of Notre Dame Press, 1968; shows immigrants in anthracite field helped build unionism.

28. Grossman, Jonathan, *William Sylvis* Columbia University Press, 1945.

29. Harvey, Katherine S. *The Best Dressed Miners: Maryland Coal Region 1835-1910* Cornell University Press, 1969.

30. Haywood, William D. *Bill Haywood's Book,* International Publishers, 1929, includes recollections as as secretary WFM, later IWW.

31. Jensen, Vernon H., *Heritage of Conflict,* Cornell University Press, 1950. The basic history of the Western Federation of Miners.

32. Jones, Sinclair Snow, *Pan-American Labor Federation,* Duke University Press, 1964.

33. Keiser, John H., "The Union Miners' Cemetery at Mt. Olive, Illinois" in *Journal of Illinois State Historical Society,* Autumn 1969.

34. Lane, Winthrop D., *Civil War in West Virginia,* Huebsch 1921, Arno reprint 1971. Depicts life where company is judge and landlord.

35. Marcus, Irwin M., "Labor Discontent in Tioga County, Pa., 1865-1905" in *Labor History,* Summer, 1973; the setting of the Arnot strike.

36. McGovern, George S. (with Leonard Guttridge) *The Great Coalfield War,* Houghton-Mifflin, 1972, an elaboration of his 1953 doctoral dissertation on Colorado strike 1913-1914. Very detailed account of Ludlow; includes account of 1903-04 coal strike; very readable.

37. McLean, Lois C., "Mother Jones.. The Miner's Striking Spirit" in *The Pittsburgh Press,* Jan. 20, 1974. I am indebted to Mrs. McLean for much data from her still incomplete biography of Mother Jones, and have indicated such sources as "37-A".

38. Michelson, Miriam, "Sweet Land of Liberty", illustrated article on W. Virginia strike in *Everybody's Magazine,* May 1913, 13 pp.

39. Michelson, Peter C., "Mother Jones" in *Delineator,* May, 1915, a one page article, undocumented, source of many uncertain bits in the Mother Jones legend.

40. Mikeal, Judith Elaine, "Mother Jones: The Labor Movement's Impious Joan of Arc", unpublished MA thesis, History, University of North Carolina, 1965: Along with Raffaele's, the pioneer serious study of Mother Jones.

41. Mooney, Fred, *Struggle in the Coal Fields,* Morgantown: West Virginia University Library, 1967. First hand account of Dist. 17 union struggles and 1921 trip to Mexico with Mother Jones.

42. Perlman, Selig and Taft, Philip, *A History of Trade Unionism in the United States, 1896-1932* originally Vol. IV of same title by Commons and Associates; Kelly reprint 1950. This volume more than any other single volume will provide the general labor history background of the Mother Jones story.

43. Powderly, Terence V., *The Path I Trod,* Columbia University Press, 1940.

44. Raffaele, Sister John Francis, GNSA, "Mary Harris Jones and the United Mine Workers" MA thesis, Catholic University of America, Aug. 1969; based primarily on UMW Journal and UMWA records.

45. Sinclair, Upton B. *King Coal,* McMillan, 1917. A novel on Ludlow etc.

46. Smith, Russel E., "The March of the Mill Children" in Social Service Review, Vol. 41, Sept. 1, 1967, on the 1903 demonstration.

47. Steel, Edward. "Mother Jones in the Fairmont Field, 1902" in *Journal of American History,* Vol. 57, Sept. 1970.

48. Stone, Irving, *"Clarence Darrow for the Defense",* 1941; a breezy biography with vivid descriptions of anthracite situation 1902, and other labor cases in which Mother Jones was involved.

49. Suggs, George G. Jr., *Colorado's War on Militant Unionism,* Wayne University Press, 1972. Major study of the 1902-1904 effort to crush unionism as part of NAM drive.

50. Taft, Philip, "The Bisbee Deportation" in *Labor History* Winter, 1972.

51. Tippet, Thomas, *Horse Shoe Bottoms,* Harper, 1935, a novel about Illinois mining last century.

52. Thompson, Fred, *The IWW: Its First 50 Years,* IWW Chicago 1955.

53. Todes, Charlotte, *William H. Sylvis and the National Labor Union,* International Publishers, 1942.

54. U.S. Commission on Industrial Relations *Final Report and Testimony,* Senate Document 215, 64th Congress, 1st Session 1916; Mother Jones' testimony is in Volume 11.

55. Van Tine, Warren R., *The Making of the Labor Bureaucrat, 1870-1920,* University of Massachusetts Press, 1973; how growth of national market reshaped union structures and policy.

56. Vorse, Mary Heaton, *Men and Steel,* Boni & Liverright, 1920.

57. Ward, Robert D., and Roger W.W., *Labor Revolt in Alabama, 1894,* University of Alabama Press, 1964.

58. Ware, Norman J., *The Labor Movement in the United States 1860-1895,* includes clear account of Knights of Labor.

59. Warne, Colston E., *The Pullman Boycott of 1894,* Heath, 1955.

60. West, Harold E., "Civil War in West Virginia Coal Mines" in *Survey,* April 1913, Vol. 30, pages 35-50; a comprehensive account of the 1912-1913 conflict by the Baltimore Sun reporter who accompanied Mother Jones to Wineburg. Illustrated.

61. Werstein, Irving, *Labor's Defiant Lady,* Crowell, 1969, story of Mother Jones for young readers.

62. Wiebe, Robert, "The Anthracite Strike of 1902" in *Mississippi Valley Historical Review,* Sept. 1961.

ADDENDA, 1980

Later general accounts of Mother Jones include Priscilla Long's *Mother Jones, Woman Organizer* (44 pages, Red Sun Press, Cambridge, 1976); Linda Atkinson's *Mother Jones, The Most Dangerous Woman in America* (for grade 6 and adults, many good photos, 240 pp, Crown 1978); chapters in Judith Nies' *Seven Women: Portraits from the American Radical Tradition* (Viking, 1977, well researched) and in *Women Who Fought,* published by the authors, Gail Reifert and Eugene Dermody at Cerritos College, Norwalk, CA, 1978. Pat Creech Sholten studies Mother Jones' oratory in her Ph. D. dissertation "Militant Women for Economic Justice" (Indiana University, Bloomington, Speech, 1978).

On the 1897 strike at Lattimer there are Michael Novak's *The Guns of Lattimer* (Basic Books, 1978) and Howard Pinkowsky's *Lattimer Massacre* (Sunshine Press, 1950). James Morris details the unfulfilled plan to buy Mitchell a home (denounced by Mother Jones page 88) in his "Acquisitive Spirit of John Mitchell", *Labor History,* Winter, 1979. Daniel Jordan describes the Mingo war of 1921 and David Corbin writes on Frank Mooney in *Essays in Southern Labor History* (Greenwood, 1977). Wallace Knight describes Gov. Hatfield's visit as doctor to his prisoner, Mother Jones, in the *Atlantic,* August 1976. Stuart Sprague writes on the Paint and Cabin Creek campaigns in *West Virginia History,* April 1977.

Dr. Howard Steale is preparing a volume of Mother Jones' letters. Lois McLean continues her research toward a definitive biography and in *Goldenseal* Jan-March, 1980 published Monia Baumgartner's recollections of Mother Jones. The West Virginia Labor History Association observed the 50th anniversary of Mother Jones' death with a "Mother Jones' and Miners' Festival".

Several plays have been produced on Mother Jones, among them "Brimstone and Lace" by Bob and Carole Damron, "Petticoats, Principles and Perseverance" by a drama group at Circle Campus, Chicago, and in French the drama "Maman Jones". A French translation of the autobiography has been published by Maspero, and sections of it have been published in Sweden to teach English in trade union schools. Mary Settle's 1980 novel *The Scapegoat* (Random House) features Mother Jones.

FOREWORD

Mother Jones is one of the most forceful and picturesque figures of the American labor movement. She is a born crusader. In an earlier period of the world she would have joined with Peter the Hermit in leading the crusaders against the Saracens. At a later period, she would have joined John Brown in his mad, heroic effort to liberate the slaves. Like Brown, she has a singleness of purpose, a personal fearlessness and a contempt for established wrongs. Like him the purpose was the moving force, and the means of accomplishing the end did not matter.

In her early life, she found in the labor movement an outlet for her inherent sympathy and love and daring. She never had the time or the education to study the philosophy of the various movements that from time to time have inspired the devoted idealist to lead what seemed to be a forlorn hope to change the institutions of men.

Mother Jones is essentially an individualist. Her own emotions and ideas are so strong that she is sometimes in conflict with others, fighting for the same cause. This too is an old story; the real leaders of any cause are necessarily individualists and are often impatient of others who likewise must go in their own way. All movements attract men and women of various minds. The early abolitionists could not agree as to methods. In their crusade were found the men who believed in constitutional methods, such as Giddings and Lincoln; the men who believed in force, of which John Brown was the chief; the non-resistant, like William Lloyd Garrison; the lone individualist who hit wherever he found a head to hit, like Wendell Phillips. Mother Jones is the Wendell Phillips of the labor movement. Without his educations and scholarship, she has the power of moving masses of men by her strong, living speech and action. She has likewise his disregard for personal safety. After the capture of John Brown at Harper's Ferry, many real abolitionists were paralyzed with fear and fled from the field, but Wendell Phillips hurled his philippics from the house-tops and defied his enemies to do their worst.

In all her career, Mother Jones never quailed or ran away. Her deep convictions and fearless soul always drew her to seek the spot where the fight was hottest and the danger greatest.

I never personally knew anything of her misunderstandings with John Mitchell, but it seems only fair for me to say that I was associated with him for many months in the arbitration growing out of the coal strike. We were friends for many years and he always had my full respect and trust. I cannot help feeling that both were true and that the disagreements were only such as inevitably grow out of close association of different types of mind in a great conflict.

Mother Jones was always doubtful of the good of organized institutions. These require compromises and she could not compromise. To her there was but one side. Right and wrong were forever distinct. The type is common to all great movements. It is essentially the difference between the man of action and the philosopher. Both are useful. No one can decide the relative merits of the two.

This little book is a story of a woman of action fired by a fine zeal. She defied calumny. She was not awed by guns or jails. She kept on her way regardless of friends and foes. She had but one love to which she was always true and that was her cause. People of this type are bound to have conflicts within and without the ranks.

Mother Jones was especially devoted to the miners. The mountainous country, the deep mines, the black pit, the cheap homes, the danger, the everlasting conflict for wages and for life, appealed to her imagination and chivalry. Much of the cause of trades unionism in England and America has been associated with the mines. The stories of the work of women and children in the mines of Great Britain are well known to all trades unionists. The progress of trades unionism in England was largely the progress of the miners' cause. The fight in America has been almost a replica of the contest in Great Britain. Through suffering, danger and loyalty the condition of the miners has gradually improved. Some of the fiercest combats in America have been fought by the miners. These fights brought thousands of men and their families close to starvation. They brought contests with police, militia, courts and soldiers. They involved prison sentences, massacres and hardships without end. Wherever the fight was the fiercest, Mother Jones was present to aid and cheer. In both the day and the night, in the poor villages and at the lonely cabin on the mountain side, Mother Jones always appeared in time of need. She had a strong sense of drama. She staged every detail of a contest. Her actors were real men and women and children, and she often reached the hearts of employers where all others failed. She was never awed by jails. Over and over she was sentenced by courts; she never ran away. She stayed in prison until her enemies opened the doors. Her personal non--resistance was far more powerful than any appeal to force.

This little book gives her own story of an active, dramatic life. It is a part of the history of the labor movement of the United States.

CLARENCE DARROW.

Chicago, June 6th, 1925.

XLV

Mother Jones in 1925

XLVI

THE AUTOBIOGRAPHY OF MOTHER JONES

CHAPTER I

EARLY YEARS

I was born in the city of Cork, Ireland, in 1830. My people were poor. For generations they had fought for Ireland's freedom. Many of my folks have died in that struggle. My father, Richard Harris, came to America in 1835, and as soon as he had become an American citizen he sent for his family. His work as a laborer with railway construction crews took him to Toronto, Canada. Here I was brought up but always as the child of an American citizen. Of that citizenship I have ever been proud.

After finishing the common schools, I attended the Normal school with the intention of becoming a teacher. Dress-making too, I learned proficiently. My first position was teaching in a convent in Monroe, Michigan. Later, I came to Chicago and opened a dress-making establishment. I preferred sewing to bossing little children.

However, I went back to teaching again, this

time in Memphis, Tennessee. Here I was married in 1861. My husband was an iron moulder and a staunch member of the Iron Moulders' Union.

In 1867, a yellow fever epidemic swept Memphis. Its victims were mainly among the poor and the workers. The rich and the well-to-do fled the city. Schools and churches were closed. People were not permitted to enter the house of a yellow fever victim without permits. The poor could not afford nurses. Across the street from me, ten persons lay dead from the plague. The dead surrounded us. They were buried at night quickly and without ceremony. All about my house I could hear weeping and the cries of delirium. One by one, my four little children sickened and died. I washed their little bodies and got them ready for burial. My husband caught the fever and died. I sat alone through nights of grief. No one came to me. No one could. Other homes were as stricken as was mine. All day long, all night long, I heard the grating of the wheels of the death cart.

After the union had buried my husband, I got a permit to nurse the sufferers. This I did until the plague was stamped out.

I returned to Chicago and went again into the dressmaking business with a partner. We were located on Washington Street near the lake. We worked for the aristocrats of Chi-

cago, and I had ample opportunity to observe
the luxury and extravagance of their lives.
Often while sewing for the lords and barons
who lived in magnificent houses on the Lake
Shore Drive, I would look out of the plate glass
windows and see the poor, shivering wretches,
jobless and hungry, walking along the frozen
lake front. The contrast of their condition with
that of the tropical comfort of the people for
whom I sewed was painful to me. My employers
seemed neither to notice nor to care.

Summers, too, from the windows of the rich,
I used to watch the mothers come from the west
side slums, lugging babies and little children,
hoping for a breath of cool, fresh air from the
lake. At night, when the tenements were stif-
ling hot, men, women and little children slept
in the parks. But the rich, having donated to
the charity ice fund, had, by the time it was hot
in the city, gone to seaside and mountains.

In October, 1871, the great Chicago fire
burned up our establishment and everything
that we had. The fire made thousands homeless.
We stayed all night and the next day without
food on the lake front, often going into the lake
to keep cool. Old St. Mary's church at Wabash
Avenue and Peck Court was thrown open to the
refugees and there I camped until I could find
a place to go.

Near by in an old, tumbled down, fire
scorched building the Knights of Labor held

meetings. The Knights of Labor was the labor organization of those days. I used to spend my evenings at their meetings, listening to splendid speakers. Sundays we went out into the woods and held meetings.

Those were the days of sacrifice for the cause of labor. Those were the days when we had no halls, when there were no high salaried officers, no feasting with the enemies of labor. Those were the days of the martyrs and the saints.

I became acquainted with the labor movement. I learned that in 1865, after the close of the Civil War, a group of men met in Louisville, Kentucky. They came from the North and from the South; they were the "blues" and the "greys" who a year or two before had been fighting each other over the question of chattel slavery. They decided that the time had come to formulate a program to fight another brutal form of slavery—industrial slavery. Out of this decision had come the Knights of Labor.

From the time of the Chicago fire I became more and more engrossed in the labor struggle and I decided to take an active part in the efforts of the working people to better the conditions under which they worked and lived. I became a member of the Knights of Labor.

One of the first strikes that I remember occurred in the Seventies. The Baltimore and Ohio Railroad employees went on strike and they sent for me to come help them. I went.

The mayor of Pittsburgh swore in as deputy sheriffs a lawless, reckless bunch of fellows who had drifted into that city during the panic of 1873. They pillaged and burned and rioted and looted. Their acts were charged up to the striking workingmen. The governor sent the militia.

The Railroads had succeeded in getting a law passed that in case of a strike, the train-crew should bring in the locomotive to the round-house before striking. This law the strikers faithfully obeyed. Scores of locomotives were housed in Pittsburgh.

One night a riot occurred. Hundreds of box cars standing on the tracks were soaked with oil and set on fire and sent down the tracks to the roundhouse. The roundhouse caught fire. Over one hundred locomotives, belonging to the Pennsylvania Railroad Company were destroyed. It was a wild night. The flames lighted the sky and turned to fiery flames the steel bayonettes of the soldiers.

The strikers were charged with the crimes of arson and rioting, although it was common knowledge that it was not they who instigated the fire; that it was started by hoodlums backed by the business men of Pittsburgh who for a long time had felt that the Railroad Company discriminated against their city in the matter of rates.

I knew the strikers personally. I knew that

it was they who had tried to enforce orderly
law. I knew they disciplined their members
when they did violence. I knew, as everybody
knew, who really perpetrated the crime of burning the railroad's property. Then and there I
learned in the early part of my career that labor
must bear the cross for others' sins, must be
the vicarious sufferer for the wrongs that
others do.

These early years saw the beginning of
America's industrial life. Hand and hand with
the growth of factories and the expansion of
railroads, with the accumulation of capital and
the rise of banks, came anti-labor legislation.
Came strikes. Came violence. Came the belief
in the hearts and minds of the workers that
legislatures but carry out the will of the industrialists.

CHAPTER II

The Haymarket Tragedy

From 1880 on, I became wholly engrossed in the labor movement. In all the great industrial centers the working class was in rebellion. The enormous immigration from Europe crowded the slums, forced down wages and threatened to destroy the standard of living fought for by American working men. Throughout the country there was business depression and much unemployment. In the cities there was hunger and rags and despair.

Foreign agitators who had suffered under European despots preached various schemes of economic salvation to the workers. The workers asked only for bread and a shortening of the long hours of toil. The agitators gave them visions. The police gave them clubs.

Particularly the city of Chicago was the scene of strike after strike, followed by boycotts and riots. The years preceeding 1886 had witnessed strikes of the lake seamen, of dock laborers and street railway workers. These strikes had been brutally suppressed by policemen's clubs and by hired gunmen. The grievance on the part of the workers was given no heed. John Bonfield, inspector of police, was particularly cruel in the suppression of meetings where men peacefully assembled to discuss matters of wages and of hours. Employers were defiant and open in the expression of their fears and hatreds. The Chicago Tribune, the organ of the employers, suggested ironically that the farmers of Illinois treat the tramps that poured out of the great industrial centers as they did other pests, by putting strychnine in the food.

The workers started an agitation for an eight-hour day. The trades unions and the Knights of Labor endorsed the movement but because many of the leaders of the agitation were foreigners, the movement itself was regarded as "foreign" and as "un-American." Then the anarchists of Chicago, a very small group, espoused the cause of the eight-hour day. From then on the people of Chicago seemed incapable of discussing a purely economic question without getting excited about anarchism.

The employers used the cry of anarchism to kill the movement. A person who believed in an eight-hour working day was, they said, an enemy to his country, a traitor, an anarchist. The foundations of government were being gnawed away by the anarchist rats. Feeling was bitter. The city was divided into two angry camps. The working people on one side—hungry, cold, jobless, fighting gunmen and

police clubs with bare hands. On the other side
the employers, knowing neither hunger nor
cold, supported by the newspapers, by the
police, by all the power of the great state itself.

The anarchists took advantage of the widespread discontent to preach their doctrines.
Orators used to address huge crowds on the
windy, barren shore of Lake Michigan. Although I never endorsed the philosophy of anarchism, I often attended the meetings on the
lake shore, listening to what these teachers of
a new order had to say to the workers.

Meanwhile the employers were meeting.
They met in the mansion of George M. Pullman
on Prairie Avenue or in the residence of Wirt
Dexter, an able corporation lawyer. They discussed means of killing the eight-hour movement which was to be ushered in by a general
strike. They discussed methods of dispersing
the meetings of the anarchists.

A bitterly cold winter set in. Long unemployment resulted in terrible suffering. Bread
lines increased. Soup kitchens could not handle
the applicants. Thousands knew actual misery.

On Christmas day, hundreds of poverty
stricken people in rags and tatters, in thin
clothes, in wretched shoes paraded on fashionable Prairie Avenue before the mansions of the
rich, before their employers, carrying the black
flag. I thought the parade an insane move on
the part of the anarchists, as it only served to

make feeling more bitter. As a matter of fact, it had no educational value whatever and only served to increase the employers' fear, to make the police more savage, and the public less sympathetic to the real distress of the workers.

The first of May, which was to usher in the eight-hour day uprising, came. The newspapers had done everything to alarm the people. All over the city there were strikes and walkouts. Employers quaked in their boots. They saw revolution. The workers in the McCormick Harvester Works gathered outside the factory. Those inside who did not join the strikers were called scabs. Bricks were thrown. Windows were broken. The scabs were threatened. Some one turned in a riot call.

The police without warning charged down upon the workers, shooting into their midst, clubbing right and left. Many were trampled under horses' feet. Numbers were shot dead. Skulls were broken. Young men and young girls were clubbed to death.

The Pinkerton agency formed armed bands of ex-convicts and hoodlums and hired them to capitalists at eight dollars a day, to picket the factories and incite trouble.

On the evening of May 4th, the anarchists held a meeting in the shabby, dirty district known to later history as Haymarket Square. All about were railway tracks, dingy saloons and the dirty tenements of the poor. A half

a block away was the Desplaines Street Police
Station presided over by John Bonfield, a man
without tact or discretion or sympathy, a most
brutal believer in suppression as the method to
settle industrial unrest.

Carter Harrison, the mayor of Chicago, attended the meeting of the anarchists and moved
in and about the crowds in the square. After
leaving, he went to the Chief of Police and in-
structed him to send no mounted police to the
meeting, as it was being peacefully conducted
and the presence of mounted police would only
add fuel to fires already burning red in the
workers' hearts. But orders perhaps came
from other quarters, for disregarding the
report of the mayor, the chief of police sent
mounted policemen in large numbers to the
meeting.

One of the anarchist speakers was addressing the crowd. A bomb was dropped from a
window overlooking the square. A number of
the police were killed in the explosion that followed.

The city went insane and the newspapers did
everything to keep it like a madhouse. The
workers' cry for justice was drowned in the
shriek for revenge. Bombs were "found"
every five minutes. Men went armed and gun
stores kept open nights. Hundreds were arrested. Only those who had agitated for an
eight-hour day, however, were brought to trial

and a few months later hanged. But the man, Schnaubelt, who actually threw the bomb was never brought into the case, nor was his part in the terrible drama ever officially made clear.

The leaders in the eight hour day movement were hanged Friday, November the 11th. That day Chicago's rich had chills and fever. Ropes stretched in all directions from the jail. Police men were stationed along the ropes armed with riot rifles. Special patrols watched all approaches to the jail. The roofs about the grim stone building were black with police. The newspapers fed the public imagination with stories of uprisings and jail deliveries.

But there were no uprisings, no jail deliveries, except that of Louis Lingg, the only real preacher of violence among all the condemned men. He outwitted the gallows by biting a percussion cap and blowing off his head.

The Sunday following the executions, the funerals were held. Thousands of workers marched behind the black hearses, not because they were anarchists but they felt that these men, whatever their theories, were martyrs to the workers' struggle. The procession wound through miles and miles of streets densely packed with silent people.

In the cemetery of Waldheim, the dead were buried. But with them was not buried their cause. The struggle for the eight hour day, for more human conditions and relations between man and man lived on, and still lives on.

Seven years later, Governor Altgeld, after reading all the evidence in the case, pardoned the three anarchists who had escaped the gallows and were serving life sentences in jail. He said the verdict was unjustifiable, as had William Dean Howells and William Morris at the time of its execution. Governor Altgeld committed political suicide by his brave action but he is remembered by all those who love truth and those who have the courage to confess it.

CHAPTER III

A STRIKE IN VIRGINIA

It was about 1891 when I was down in Virginia. There was a strike in the Dietz mines and the boys had sent for me. When I got off the train at Norton a fellow walked up to me and asked me if I were Mother Jones.

"Yes, I am Mother Jones."

He looked terribly frightened. "The superintendent told me that if you came down here he would blow out your brains. He said he didn't want to see you 'round these parts."

"You tell the superintendent that I am not coming to see him anyway. I am coming to see the miners."

As we stood talking a poor fellow, all skin and bones, joined us.

"Do you see those cars over there, Mother, on the siding?" He pointed to cars filled with coal.

"Well, we made a contract with the coal company to fill those cars for so much, and after we had made the contract, they put lower bottoms in the cars, so that they would hold another ton or so. I have worked for this company all my life and all I have now is this old worn-out frame."

We couldn't get a hall to hold a meeting. Every one was afraid to rent to us. Finally the colored people consented to give us their church for our meeting. Just as we were about to start the colored chairman came to me and said: "Mother, the coal company gave us this ground that the church is on. They have sent word that they will take it from us if we let you speak here."

I would not let those poor souls lose their ground so I adjourned the meeting to the four corners of the public roads. When the meeting was over and the people had dispersed, I asked my co-worker, Dud Hado, a fellow from Iowa, if he would go with me up to the post office. He was a kindly soul but easily frightened.

As we were going along the road, I said, "Have you got a pistol on you?"

"Yes," said he, "I'm not going to let any one blow your brains out."

"My boy," said I, it is against the law in this county to carry concealed weapons. I want you to take that pistol out and expose a couple of inches of it."

As he did so about eight or ten gunmen jumped out from behind an old barn beside the road, jumped on him and said, "Now we've got you, you dirty organizer." They bullied us along the road to the town and we were taken to an office where they had a notary public

and we were tried. All those blood-thirsty
murderers were there and the general manager
came in.

"Mother Jones, I am astonished," said he.

"What is your astonishment about?" said I.

"That you should go into the house of God
with anyone who carries a gun."

"Oh that wasn't God's house," said I. "That
is the coal company's house. Don't you know
that God Almighty never comes around to a
place like this!"

He laughed and of course, the dogs laughed,
for he was the general manager.

They dismissed any charges against me and
they fined poor Dud twenty-five dollars and
costs. They seemed surprised when I said I
would pay it. I had the money in my petticoat.

I went over to a miner's shack and asked his
wife for a cup of tea. Often in these company-
owned towns the inn-keepers were afraid to let
me have food. The poor soul was so happy to
have me there that she excused herself to
"dress for company." She came out of the
bedroom with a white apron on over her cheap
cotton wrapper.

One of the men who was present at Dud's
trial followed me up to the miner's house. At
first the miner's wife would not admit him but
he said he wanted to speak privately to Mother
Jones. So she let him in.

"Mother," he said, "I am glad you paid that

bill so quickly. They thought you'd appeal the
case. Then they were going to lock you both
up and burn you in the coke ovens at night and
then say that you had both been turned loose
in the morning and they didn't know where you
had gone.''

Whether they really would have carried out
their plans I do not know. But I do know that
there are no limits to which powers of privilege
will not go to keep the workers in slavery.

CHAPTER IV

WAYLAND'S APPEAL TO REASON

In 1893, J. A. Wayland with a number of others decided to demonstrate to the workers the advantage of co-operation over competition. A group of people bought land in Tennessee and founded the Ruskin Colony. They invited me to join them.

"No," said I, "your colony will not succeed. You have to have religion to make a colony successful, and labor is not yet a religion with labor."

I visited the colony a year later. I could see in that short time disrupting elements in the colony. I was glad I had not joined the colony but had stayed out in the thick of the fight. Labor has a lot of fighting to do before it can demonstrate. Two years later Wayland left for Kansas City. He was despondent.

A group of us got together; Wayland, myself, and three men, known as the "Three P's" —Putnam, a freight agent for the Burlington Railway; Palmer, a clerk in the Post Office; Page, an advertising agent for a department store. We decided that the workers needed education. That they must have a paper devoted to their interests and stating their point of view. We urged Wayland to start such a paper. Palmer suggested the name, "Appeal to Reason."

"But we have no subscribers," said Wayland.

"I'll get them," said I. "Get out your first edition and I'll see that it has subscribers enough to pay for it."

He got out a limited first edition and with it as a sample I went to the Federal Barracks at Omaha and secured a subscription from almost every lad there. Soldiers are the sons of working people and need to know it. I went down to the City Hall and got a lot of subscriptions. In a short time I had gathered several hundred subscriptions and the paper was launched. It did a wonderful service under Wayland. Later Fred G. Warren came to Girard where the paper was published, as editorial writer. If any place in America could be called my home, his home was mine. Whenever, after a long, dangerous fight, I was weary and felt the need of rest, I went to the home of Fred Warren.

Like all other things, "The Appeal to Reason" had its youth of vigor, its later days of profound wisdom, and then it passed away. Disrupting influences, quarrels, divergent points of view, theories, finally caused it to go out of business.

CHAPTER V

Victory at Arnot

Beforre 1899 the coal fields of Pennsylvania were not organized. Immigrants poured into the country and they worked cheap. There was always a surplus of immigrant labor, solicited in Europe by the coal companies, so as to keep wages down to barest living. Hours of work down under ground were cruelly long. Fourteen hours a day was not uncommon, thirteen, twelve. The life or limb of the miner was unprotected by any laws. Families lived in company owned shacks that were not fit for their pigs. Children died by the hundreds due to the ignorance and poverty of their parents.

Often I have helped lay out for burial the babies of the miners, and the mothers could scarce conceal their relief at the little ones' deaths. Another was already on its way, destined, if a boy, for the breakers; if a girl, for the silk mills where the other brothers and sisters already worked.

The United Mine Workers decided to organize these fields and work for human conditions for human beings. Organizers were put to work. Whenever the spirit of the men in the mines grew strong enough a strike was called.

In Arnot, Pennsylvania, a strike had been going on four or five months. The men were becoming discouraged. The coal company sent the doctors, the school teachers, the preachers and their wives to the homes of the miners to get them to sign a document that they would go back to work.

The president of the district, Mr. Wilson, and an organizer, Tom Haggerty, got despondent. The signatures were overwhelmingly in favor of returning on Monday.

Haggerty suggested that they send for me. Saturday morning they telephoned to Barnesboro, where I was organizing, for me to come at once or they would lose the strike.

"Oh Mother," Haggerty said, "Come over quick and help us! The boys are that despondent! They are going back Monday."

I told him that I was holding a meeting that night but that I would leave early Sunday morning.

I started at daybreak. At Roaring Branch, the nearest train connection with Arnot, the secretary of the Arnot Union, a young boy, William Bouncer, met me with a horse and buggy. We drove sixteen miles over rough mountain roads. It was biting cold. We got into Arnot Sunday noon and I was placed in the coal company's hotel, the only hotel in town. I made some objections but Bouncer said, "Mother, we have engaged this room for you and if it is not occupied, they will never rent us another.''

Sunday afternoon I held a meeting. It was not as large a gathering as those we had later but I stirred up the poor wretches that did come.

"You've got to take the pledge," I said. "Rise and pledge to stick to your brothers and the union till the strike's won!"

The men shuffled their feet but the women rose, their babies in their arms, and pledged themselves to see that no one went to work in the morning.

"The meeting stands adjourned till ten o'clock tomorrow morning," I said. "Everyone come and see that the slaves that think to go back to their masters come along with you."

I returned to my room at the hotel. I wasn't called down to supper but after the general manager of the mines and all of the other guests had gone to church, the housekeeper stole up to my room and asked me to come down and get a cup of tea.

At eleven o'clock that night the housekeeper again knocked at my door and told me that I had to give up my room; that she was told it belonged to a teacher. "It's a shame, mother," she whispered, as she helped me into my coat.

I found little Bouncer sitting on guard down in the lobby. He took me up the mountain to a miner's house. A cold wind almost blew the bonnet from my head. At the miner's shack I knocked.

A man's voice shouted, "Who is there?"

"Mother Jones," said I.

A light came in the tiny window. The door opened.

"And did they put you out, Mother?"

"They did that."

"I told Mary they might do that," said the miner. He held the oil lamp with the thumb and his little finger and I could see that the others were off. His face was young but his body was bent over.

He insisted on my sleeping in the only bed, with his wife. He slept with his head on his arms on the kitchen table. Early in the morning his wife rose to keep the children quiet, so that I might sleep a little later as I was very tired.

At eight o'clock she came into my room, crying.

"Mother, are you awake?"

"Yes, I am awake."

"Well, you must get up. The sheriff is here to put us out for keeping you. This house belongs to the Company."

The family gathered up all their earthly belongings, which weren't much, took down all the holy pictures, and put them in a wagon, and they with all their neighbors went to the meeting. The sight of that wagon with the sticks of furniture and the holy pictures and the children, with the father and mother and myself walking along through the streets turned the tide. It made the men so angry that they decided not to go back that morning to the mines. Instead they came to the meeting where they determined not to give up the strike until they had won the victory.

Then the company tried to bring in scabs. I told the men to stay home with the children for a change and let the women attend to the scabs. I organized an army of women housekeepers. On a given day they were to bring their mops and brooms and "the army" would charge the scabs up at the mines. The general manager, the sheriff and the corporation hirelings heard of our plans and were on hand. The day came and the women came with the mops and brooms and pails of water.

I decided not to go up to the Drip Mouth myself, for I knew they would arrest me and that might rout the army. I selected as leader an Irish woman who had a most picturesque appearance. She had slept late and her husband had told her to hurry up and get into the army. She had grabbed a red petticoat and slipped it over a thick cotton night gown. She wore a black stocking and a white one. She had tied a little red fringed shawl over her wild red hair. Her face was red and her eyes were mad. I looked at her and felt that she could raise a rumpus.

I said, "You lead the army up to the Drip Mouth. Take that tin dishpan you have with you and your hammer, and when the scabs and the mules come up, begin to hammer and howl. Then all of you hammer and howl and be ready to chase the scabs with your mops and brooms. Don't be afraid of anyone."

Up the mountain side, yelling and hollering, she led the women, and when the mules came up with the scabs and the coal, she began beating on the dishpan and hollering and all the army joined in with her. The sheriff tapped her on the shoulder.

"My dear lady," said he, "remember the mules. Don't frighten them."

She took the old tin pan and she hit him with it and she hollered, "To hell with you and the mules!"

He fell over and dropped into the creek. Then the mules began to rebel against scabbing. They bucked and kicked the scab drivers and started off for the barn. The scabs started running down hill, followed by the army of women with their mops and pails and brooms.

A poll parrot in a near by shack screamed at the superintendent, "Got hell, did you? Got hell?"

There was a great big doctor in the crowd, a company lap dog. He had a little satchel in his hand and he said to me, impudent like, "Mrs. Jones, I have a warrant for you."

"All right," said I. "Keep it in your pill bag until I come for it. I am going to hold a meeting now."

From that day on the women kept continual watch of the mines to see that the company did not bring in scabs. Every day women with brooms or mops in one hand and babies in the other arm wrapped in little blankets, went to the mines and watched that no one went in. And all night long they kept watch. They were heroic women. In the long years to come the nation will pay them high tribute for they were fighting for the advancement of a great country.

I held meetings throughout the surrounding country. The company was spending money among the farmers, urging them not to do anything for the miners. I went out with an old wagon and a union mule that had gone on strike, and a miner's little boy for a driver. I held meetings among the farmers and won them to the side of the strikers.

Sometimes it was twelve or one o'clock in the morning when I would get home, the little boy asleep on my arm and I driving the mule. Sometimes it was several degrees below zero. The winds whistled down the mountains and drove the snow and sleet in our faces. My hands and feet were often numb. We were all living on dry bread and black coffee. I slept in a room that never had a fire in it, and I often woke up in the morning to find snow covering the outside covers of the bed.

There was a place near Arnot called Sweedy Town, and the company's agents went there to get the Swedes to break the strike. I was holding a meeting among the farmers when I heard of the company's efforts. I got the young farmers to get on their horses and go over to Sweedy Town and see that no Swede left town. They took clotheslines for lassos and any Swede seen moving in the direction of Arnot was brought back quick enough.

After months of terrible hardships the strike was about won. The mines were not working. The spirit of the men was splendid. President Wilson had come home from the western part of the state. I was staying at his home. The family had gone to bed. We sat up late talking over matters when there came a knock at the door. A very cautious knock.

"Come in," said Mr. Wilson.

Three men entered. They looked at me uneasily and Mr. Wilson asked me to step in an adjoining room. They talked the strike over and called President Wilson's attention to the fact that there were mortgages on his little home, held by the bank which was owned by the coal company, and they said, "We will take the mortgage off your home and give you

$25,000 in cash if you will just leave and let the strike die out.''

I shall never forget his reply:

"Gentlemen, if you come to visit my family, the hospitality of the whole house is yours. But if you come to bribe me with dollars to betray my manhood and my brothers who trust me, I want you to leave this door and never come here again.''

The strike lasted a few weeks longer. Meantime President Wilson, when strikers were evicted, cleaned out his barn and took care of the evicted miners until homes could be provided. One by one he killed his chickens and his hogs. Everything that he had he shared. He ate dry bread and drank chicory. He knew every hardship that the rank and file of the organization knew. We do not have such leaders now.

The last of February the company put up a notice that all demands were conceded.

"Did you get the use of the hall for us to hold meetings?" said the women.

"No, we didn't ask for that.''

"Then the strike is on again," said they.

They got the hall, and when the President, Mr. Wilson, returned from the convention in Cincinnati he shed tears of joy and gratitude.

I was going to leave for the central fields, and before I left, the union held a victory meeting in Bloosburg. The women came for miles

in a raging snow storm for that meeting, little
children trailing on their skirts, and babies
under their shawls. Many of the miners had
walked miles. It was one night of real joy and
a great celebration. I bade them all good bye.
A little boy called out, "Don't leave us, Mother.
Don't leave us!" The dear little children
kissed my hands. We spent the whole night in
Bloosburg rejoicing. The men opened a few of
the freight cars out on a siding and helped
themselves to boxes of beer. Old and young
talked and sang all night long and to the credit
of the company no one was interfered with.

Those were the days before the extensive use
of gun men, of military, of jails, of police clubs.
There had been no bloodshed. There had been
no riots. And the victory was due to the army
of women with their mops and brooms.

A year afterward they celebrated the anniversary of the victory. They presented me with
a gold watch but I declined to accept it, for I
felt it was the price of the bread of the little
children. I have not been in Arnot since but
in my travels over the country I often meet the
men and boys who carried through the strike so
heroically.

CHAPTER VI

One night I went with an organizer named Scott to a mining town in the Fairmont district where the miners had asked me to hold a meeting. When we got off the car I asked Scott where I was to speak and he pointed to a frame building. We walked in. There were lighted candles on an altar. I looked around in the dim light. We were in a church and the benches were filled with miners.

Outside the railing of the altar was a table. At one end sat the priest with the money of the union in his hands. The president of the local union sat at the other end of the table. I marched down the aisle.

"What's going on?" I asked.

"Holding a meeting," said the president.

"What for?"

"For the union, Mother. We rented the church for our meetings."

I reached over and took the money from the priest. Then I turned to the miners.

"Boys," I said, "this is a praying institution. You should not commercialize it. Get up, every one of you and go out in the open fields."

They got up and went out and sat around in

a field while I spoke to them. The sheriff was there and he did not allow any traffic to go along the road while I was speaking. In front of us was a school house. I pointed to it and I said, "Your ancestors fought for you to have a share in that institution over there. It's yours. See the school board, and every Friday night hold your meetings there. Have your wives clean it up Saturday morning for the children to enter Monday. Your organization is not a praying institution. It's a fighting institution. It's an educational institution along industrial lines. Pray for the dead and fight like hell for the living!"

———

Tom Haggerty was in charge of the Fairmont field. One Sunday morning, the striking miners of Clarksburg started on a march to Monongha to get out the miners in the camps along the line. We camped in the open fields and held meetings on the road sides and in barns, preaching the gospel of unionism.

The Consolidated Coal Company that owns the little town of New England forbade the distribution of the notices of our meeting and arrested any one found with a notice. But we got the news around. Several of our men went into the camp. They went in twos. One pretended he was deaf and the other kept hollering in his ear as they walked around, "Mother Jones is going to have a meeting Sunday af-

ternoon outside the town on the sawdust pile.''
Then the deaf fellow would ask him what he
said and he would holler to him again. So
the word got around the entire camp and we
had a big crowd.

When the meeting adjourned, three miners
and myself set out for Fairmont City. The
miners, Jo Battley, Charlie Blakelet and Barney Rice walked but they got a little boy with a
horse and buggy to drive me over. I was to
wait for the boys just outside the town, across
the bridge, just where the interurban car
comes along.

The little lad and I drove along. It was dark
when we came in sight of the bridge which I had
to cross. A dark building stood beside the
bridge. It was the Coal Company's store. It
was guarded by gunmen. There was no light on
the bridge and there was none in the store.

A gunman stopped us. I could not see his
face.

''Who are you?'' said he.

''Mother Jones,'' said I, ''and a miner's lad.''

''So that's you, Mother Jones,'' said he rattling his gun.

''Yes, it's me,'' I said, ''and be sure you take
care of the store tonight. Tomorrow I'll have
to be hunting a new job for you.''

I got out of the buggy where the road joins
the Interurban tracks, just across the bridge.
I sent the lad home.

"When you pass my boys on the road tell them to hurry up. Tell them I'm waiting just across the bridge."

There wasn't a house in sight. The only people near were the gunmen whose dark figures I could now and then see moving on the bridge. It grew very dark. I sat on the ground, waiting. I took out my watch, lighted a match and saw that it was about time for the interurban.

Suddenly the sound of "Murder! Murder! Police! Help!" rang out through the darkness. Then the sound of running and Barney Rice came screaming across the bridge toward me. Blakley followed, running so fast his heels hit the back of his head. "Murder! Murder!" he was yelling.

I rushed toward them. "Where's Jo?" I asked.

"They're killing Jo—on the bridge—the gunmen."

At that moment the Interurban car came in sight. It would stop at the bridge. I thought of a scheme.

I ran onto the bridge, shouting, "Jo! Jo! The boys are coming. They're coming! The whole bunch's coming. The car's most here!"

Those bloodhounds for the coal company thought an army of miners was in the Interurban car. They ran for cover, barricading themselves in the company's store. They left Jo on the bridge, his head broken and the blood pouring from him. I tore my petticoat into strips, bandaged his head, helped the boys to get him on to the Interurban car, and hurried the car into Fairmont City.

We took him to the hotel and sent for a doctor who sewed up the great, open cuts in his head. I sat up all night and nursed the poor fellow. He was out of his head and thought I was his mother.

The next night Tom Haggerty and I addressed the union meeting, telling them just what had happened. The men wanted to go clean up the gunmen but I told them that would only make more trouble. The meeting adjourned in a body to go see Jo. They went up to his room, six or eight of them at a time, until they had all seen him.

We tried to get a warrant out for the arrest of the gunmen but we couldn't because the coal company controlled the judges and the courts.

Jo was not the only man who was beaten up by the gunmen. There were many and the brutalities of these bloodhounds would fill volumes.

In Clarksburg, men were threatened with death if they even billed meetings for me. But the railway men billed a meeting in the dead of night and I went in there alone. The meeting was in the court house. The place was packed. The mayor and all the city officials were there.

"Mr. Mayor," I said, "will you kindly be chairman for a fellow American citizen?"

He shook his head. No one would accept my offer.

"Then," said I, "as chairman of the evening, I introduce myself, the speaker of the evening, Mother Jones."

The Fairmont field was finally organized to a man. The scabs and the gunmen were driven out. Subsequently, through inefficient organizers, through the treachery of the unions' own officials, the unions lost strength. The miners of the Fairmont field were finally betrayed by the very men who were employed to protect their interests. Charlie Battley tried to retrieve the losses but officers had become corrupt and men so discouraged that he could do nothing.

It makes me sad indeed to think that the sacrifices men and women made to get out from under the iron heel of the gunmen were so often in vain! That the victories gained are so often destroyed by the treachery of the workers' own officials, men who themselves knew the bitterness and cost of the struggle.

I am old now and I never expect to see the boys in the Fairmont field again, but I like to think that I have had a share in changing conditions for them and for their children.

The United Mine Workers had tried to organize Kelly Creek on the Kanawah River but without results. Mr. Burke and Tom Lewis, members of the board of the United Mine Workers, decided to go look the field over for themselves. They took the train one night for Kelly Creek. The train came to a high trestle over a steep canyon. Under some pretext all the passengers except the two union officials were transferred to another coach, the coach uncoupled and pulled across the trestle. The officials were left on the trestle in the stalled car. They had to crawl on their hands and knees along the tracks. Pitch blackness was below them. The trestle was a one-way track. Just as they got to the end of the trestle, a train thundered by.

When I heard of the coal company's efforts to kill the union officers, I decided I myself must go to Kelly Creek and rouse those slaves. I took a nineteen-year-old boy, Ben Davis, with me. We walked on the east bank of the Kanawah River on which Kelly Creek is situated. Before daylight one morning, at a point opposite Kelly Creek, we forded the river.

It was just dawn when I knocked at the door of a store run by a man by the name of Marshall. I told him what I had come for. He was friendly. He took me in a little back room where he gave me breakfast. He said if anyone saw him giving food to Mother Jones he would lose his store privilege. He told me how to get my bills announcing my meeting into the mines by noon. But all the time he was frightened and kept looking out the little window.

Late that night a group of miners gathered about a mile from town between the boulders. We could not see one another's faces in the darkness. By the light of an old lantern I gave them the pledge.

The next day, forty men were discharged, blacklisted. There had been spies among the men the night before. The following night we organized another group and they were all discharged. This started the fight. Mr. Marshall, the grocery man, got courageous. He rented me his store and I began holding meetings there. The general manager for the mines came over from Columbus and he held a meeting, too.

"Shame," he said, "to be led away by an old women!"

"Hurrah for Mother Jones!" shouted the miners.

The following Sunday I held a meeting in the woods. The general manager, Mr. Jack Rowen, came down from Columbus on his special car. I organized a parade of the men that Sunday. We had every miner with us. We stood in front of the company's hotel and yelled for the general manager to come out. He did not appear. Two of the company's lap dogs were on the porch. One of them said, "I'd like to hang that old woman to a tree."

"Yes," said the other, "and I'd like to pull the rope."

On we marched to our meeting place under

the trees. Over a thousand people came and the two lap dogs came sniveling along too. I stood up to speak and I put my back to a big tree and pointing to the curs, I said, "You said that you would like to hang this old woman to a tree! Well, here's the old woman and here's the tree. Bring along your rope and hang her!"

And so the union was organized in Kelly Creek. I do not know whether the men have held the gains they wrested from the company. Taking men into the union is just the kindergarten of their education and every force is against their further education. Men who live up those lonely creeks have only the mine owners' Y. M. C. A.s, the mine owners' preachers and teachers, the mine owners' doctors and newspapers to look to for their ideas. So they don't get many.

CHAPTER VII

A HUMAN JUDGE

In June of 1902 I was holding a meeting of the bituminous miners of Clarksburg, West Virginia. I was talking on the strike question, for what else among miners should one be talking of? Nine organizers sat under a tree near by. A United States marshal notified them to tell me that I was under arrest. One of them came up to the platform.

"Mother," said he, "you're under arrest. They've got an injunction against your speaking."

I looked over at the United States marshal and I said, "I will be right with you. Wait till I run down." I went on speaking till I had finished. Then I said, "Goodbye, boys; I'm under arrest. I may have to go to jail. I may not see you for a long time. Keep up this fight! Don't surrender! Pay no attention to the injunction machine at Parkersburg. The Federal judge is a scab anyhow. While you starve he plays golf. While you serve humanity, he serves injunctions for the money powers."

That night several of the organizers and myself were taken to Parkersburg, a distance of eighty-four miles. Five deputy marshals went with the men, and a nephew of the United States marshal, a nice lad, took charge of me. On the train I got the lad very sympathetic to the cause of the miners. When we got off the train, the boys and the five marshals started off in one direction and we in the other.

"My boy," I said to my guard, "look, we are going in the wrong direction."

"No, mother," he said.

"Then they are going in the wrong direction, lad."

"No, mother. You are going to a hotel. They are going to jail."

"Lad," said I, stopping where we were, "am I under arrest?"

"You are, mother."

"Then I am going to jail with my boys." I turned square around. "Did you ever hear of Mother Jones going to a hotel while her boys were in jail?"

I quickly followed the boys and went to jail with them. But the jailer and his wife would not put me in a regular cell. "Mother," they said, "you're our guest." And they treated me as a member of the family, getting out the best of everything and "plumping me" as they called feeding me. I got a real good rest while I was with them.

We were taken to the Federal court for trial. We had violated something they called an injunction. Whatever the bosses did not want the

miners to do they got out an injunction against
doing it. The company put a woman on the
stand. She testified that I had told the miners
to go into the mines and throw out the scabs.
She was a poor skinny woman with scared eyes
and she wore her best dress, as if she were in
church. I looked at the miserable slave of the
coal company and I felt sorry for her: sorry
that there was a creature so low who would per-
jure herself for a handful of coppers.

I was put on the stand and the judge asked
me if I gave that advice to the miners, told them
to use violence.

"You know, sir," said I, "that it would be
suicidal for me to make such a statement in public. I am more careful than that. You've been
on the bench forty years, have you not, judge?"

"Yes, I have that," said he.

"And in forty years you learn to discern between a lie and the truth, judge?"

The prosecuting attorney jumped to his feet
and shaking his finger at me, he said "Your
honor, there is the most dangerous woman in
the country today. She called your honor a
scab. But I will recommend mercy of the court
if she will consent to leave the state and never
return."

"I didn't come into the court asking mercy,"
I said, "but I came here looking for justice.
And I will not leave this state so long as there is

a single little child that asks me to stay and fight his battle for bread.''

The judge said, ''Did you call me a scab?''

''I certainly did, judge.''

He said, ''How came you to call me a scab?''

''When you had me arrested I was only talking about the constitution, speaking to a lot of men about life and liberty and a chance for happiness; to men who had been robbed for years by their masters, who had been made industrial slaves. I was thinking of the immortal Lincoln. And it occurred to me that I had read in the papers that when Lincoln made the appointment of Federal judge to this bench, he did not designate senior or junior. You and your father bore the same initials. Your father was away when the appointment came. You took the appointment. Wasn't that scabbing on your father, judge?''

''I never heard that before,'' said he.

A chap came tiptoeing up to me and whispered, ''Madam, don't say 'judge' or 'sir' to the court. Say 'Your Honor.' ''

''Who is the court?'' I whispered back.

''His honor, on the bench,'' he said, looking shocked.

''Are you referring to the old chap behind the justice counter? Well, I can't call him 'your honor' until I know how honorable he is. You know I took an oath to tell the truth when I took the witness stand.''

When the court session closed I was told that
the judge wished to see me in his chambers.
When I entered the room, the judge reached out
his hand and took hold of mine, and he said,
"I wish to give you proof that I am not a scab;
that I didn't scab on my father."

He handed me documents which proved that
the reports were wrong and had been circulated
by his enemies.

"Judge," I said, "I apologize. And I am
glad to be tried by so human a judge who re-
sents being called a scab. And who would not
want to be one. You probably understand how
we working people feel about it."

He did not sentence me, just let me go, but he
gave the men who were arrested with me sixty
and ninety days in jail.

I was going to leave Parkersburg the next
night for Clarksburg. Mr. Murphy, a citizen
of Parkersburg, came to express his regrets that
I was going away. He said he was glad the
judge did not sentence me. I said to him, "If
the injunction was violated I was the only one
who violated it. The boys did not speak at all.
I regret that they had to go to jail for me and
that I should go free. But I am not trying to
break into jails. It really does not matter much;
they are young and strong and have a long time
to carry on. I am old and have much yet to do.
Only Barney Rice has a bad heart and a frail,
nervous wife. When she hears of his imprison-

ment, she may have a collapse and perhaps leave her little children without a mother's care."

Mr. Murphy said to me, "Mother Jones, I believe that if you went up and explained Rice's condition to the judge he would pardon him."

I went to the judge's house. He invited me to dinner.

"No, Judge," I said, "I just came to see you about Barney Rice."

"What about him?"

"He has heart disease and a nervous wife."

"Heart disease, has he?"

"Yes, he has it bad and he might die in your jail. I know you don't want that."

"No," replied the judge, "I do not."

He called the jailer and asked him to bring Rice to the phone. The judge said, "How is your heart, Barney?"

"Me heart's all right, all right," said Barney. "It's that damn ould judge that put me in jail for sixty days that's got something wrong wid his heart. I was just trailing around with Mother Jones."

"Nothing wrong with your heart, eh?"

"No, there ain't a damn thing wrong wid me heart! Who are you anyhow that's talking?"

"Never mind, I want to know what is the matter with your heart?"

"Hell, me heart's all right, I'm telling you."

The judge turned to me and said, "Do you hear his language?"

I told him I did not hear and he repeated to me Barney's answers. "He swears every other word," said the judge.

"Judge," said I, "that is the way we ignorant working people pray."

"Do you pray that way?"

"Yes, judge, when I want an answer quick."

"But Barney says there is nothing the matter with his heart."

"Judge, that fellow doesn't know the difference between his heart and his liver. I have been out to meetings with him and walking home down the roads or on the railroad tracks, he has had to sit down to get his breath."

The judge called the jail doctor and told him to go and examine Barney's heart in the morning. Meantime I asked my friend, Mr. Murphy, to see the jail doctor. Well, the next day Barney was let out of jail.

CHAPTER VIII

ROOSEVELT SENT FOR JOHN MITCHELL

The strike of the anthracite miners which started in the spring with $90,000 in the treasury, ended in the fall with over a million dollars in the possession of the United Mine Workers. The strike had been peaceful. The miners had the support of the public. The tie up of the colleries had been complete. Factories and railroads were without coal.

Toward fall New York began to suffer. In October, Mr. Roosevelt summoned "Divine Right Baer", President of the Coal Producers' Union, and other officials of the coal interests, to Washington. He called also the officials of the miners' union. They sat at the cabinet table, the coal officials on one side, the miners' officials at the other and the president at the head of the table in between the two groups.

They discussed the matter and the mine owners would not consent to any kind of settlement. Mr. Baer said that before he would consent to arbitration with the union he would call out the militia and shoot the miners back into the mines.

The meeting adjourned without results. Mr. Roosevelt sent for John Mitchell. He patted him on the shoulder, told him that he was the true patriot and loyal citizen and not the mine owners. After the conference there was a deadlock.

Mr. Mitchell reported the conference to the miners. They said, "All right. We have money enough to see this thing through. We will fight to a finish. Until the coal operators recognize our union and deal with our demands."

Wall Street sent for Mr. J. Pierpont Morgan to come home from Europe. He came. The situation was serious for the mine operators. The public was indignant at their stubbornness. A Mr. ———— wrote to Montgomery where I was organizing and asked me to come to New York, saying he wished to discuss the strike with me. I went to headquarters at Wilkesbarre and asked Mr. Mitchell what I should do.

He said, "Go, Mother, but whatever you do, do not consent to any outside group arbitrating this strike. The union won this strike. The operators know that they are beaten and that they must deal with the United Mine Workers."

"No," I said, "I will consent to no other group undertaking the settlement. I will report to you."

I met Mr. ———— and we went over the situation. He then went down to Mr. Morgan's office and I waited for him in his office until he returned. "Mr. Morgan is most distressed," he said on his return. "He says the miners have us!"

On Sunday afternoon, Mr. Baer and his group met on Mr. Morgan's yacht out in the bay of New York. Mr. Root came down from Washington to represent Roosevelt. Not a newspaperman was permitted out on that yacht. There were no telegrams, no telephones, no messages. How to lose the strike without apparently losing it was what they discussed. But give the victory to the union they would not!

Mr. Root proposed the way out. The President should appoint "an impartial board of inquiry." This method of settling the strike would avoid capitulation to the union, put the operators in the position of yielding to public opinion, make the miners lose public support if they refused to submit their cause to the board.

The next morning, Monday, my friend, Mr. ———, met Mr. Morgan at 209 Madison Avenue. He returned from that appointment, crying "The strike is settled."

I went back to Wilkesbarre and found that Mr. Mitchell had already been to Washington and had consented to the arbitration of the strike by a board appointed by the president.

"It would never do to refuse the president," he said, when I tried to dissuade him from taking part in the conferences.

"You have a good excuse to give the president," I replied. "Tell him that when you came home from the last conference in the cabinet room, Mr. Baer said he would shoot the miners

back before he would deal with their union.''
Tell him that the miners said, 'All right. We
will fight to a finish for the recognition of The
United Mine Workers'.''

"It would not do to tell the president that,"
he replied.

That night, Mr. Mitchell, accompanied by Mr.
Wellman, Roosevelt's publicity man, went to
Washington. He had an audience with the president the next morning. Before he left the
White House, the newspapers, magazines and
pulpits were shouting his praises, calling him
the greatest labor leader in all America. Mr.
Mitchell was not dishonest but he had a weak
point, and that was his love of flattery; and the
interests used this weak point in furtherance of
their designs.

When he returned to Wilkesbarre, priests,
ministers and politicians fell on their knees before him. Bands met him at the station. The
men took the horses from his carriage and drew
it themselves. Parades with banners marched
in his honor beside the carrriage. His black hair
was pushed back from his forehead. His face
was pale. His dark eyes shone with excitement.
There were deep lines in his face from the long
strain he had been under.

Flattery and homage did its work with John
Mitchell. The strike was won. Absolutely no
anthracite coal was being dug. The operators
could have been made to deal with the unions if

Mr. Mitchell had stood firm. A moral victory would have been won for the principle of union-ism. This to my mind was more important than the material gains which the miners received through the later decision of the president's board.

Mr. Mitchell died a rich man, distrusted by the working people whom he once served.

From out that strike came the Irish Hessian law—the establishment of a police constabulary. The bill was framed under the pretext that it would protect the farmer. Workingmen went down to Harrisburg and lobbied for it. They hated the coal and iron police of the mine own-ers and thought anything preferable to them. They forgot that the coal and iron police could join the constabulary and they forgot the his-tory of Ireland, whence the law came: Ireland, soaked with the blood of men and of women, shed by the brutal constabulary.

"No honorable man will join," said a labor leader to me when I spoke of my fears.

"Then that leaves the workers up against the bad men, the gunmen and thugs that do join," I answered.

And that's just where they have been left.

I attended the hearings of the board of in-quiry, appointed by President Roosevelt. Never shall I forget the words of John Mitchell as he appeared before the commission:

"For more than twenty years the anthracite miners have groaned under most intolerable and inhuman conditions. In a brotherhood of labor they seek to remedy their wrongs."

Never shall I forget the words of President Baer, speaking for the operators:

"The rights and interests of the laboring man will be protected not by the labor agitator but by the Christian men and women to whom God in His infinite wisdom has given the control of the property interests of this country."

Never shall I forget the words of labor's great pleader, Clarence Darrow:

"These agents of the Almighty have seen men killed daily; have seen men crippled, blinded and maimed and turned out to almshouses and on the roadsides with no compensation. They have seen the anthracite region dotted with silk mills because the wages of the miner makes it necessary for him to send his little girls to work twelve hours a day, a night, in the factory . . . at a child's wage. President Baer sheds tears because boys are taken into the union but he has no tears because they are taken into the breakers."

Never, never shall I forget his closing words, words which I shall hear when my own life draws to its close:

"This contest is one of the important contests that have marked the progress of human liberty since the world began. Every advantage that

the human race has won has been at fearful cost.
Some men must die that others may live. It
has come to these poor miners to bear this cross,
not for themselves alone but that the human
race may be lifted up to a higher and broader
plane.''

The commission found in favor of the miners
in every one of their demands. The operators
gracefully bowed to their findings. Labor
walked into the House of Victory through the
back door.

CHAPTER IX

MURDER IN WEST VIRGINIA

At the close of the anthracite strike in October, 1902, I went into the unorganized sections of West Virginia with John H. Walker of Illinois. Up and down along both sides of the New River we held meetings and organized—Smithersfield, Long Acre, Canilton, Boomer.

The work was not easy or safe and I was lucky to have so fearless a co-worker. Men who joined the union were blacklisted throughout the entire section. Their families were thrown out on the highways. Men were shot. They were beaten. Numbers disappeared and no trace of them found. Store keepers were ordered not to sell to union men or their families. Meetings had to be held in the woods at night, in abandoned mines, in barns.

We held a meeting in Mount Hope. After the meeting adjourned, Walker and I went back to our hotel. We talked till late. There came a tap on the door.

"Come in," I said.

A miner came into the room. He was lean and tall and coughed a lot.

"Mother," he said, "there are twelve of us here and we want to organize."

I turned to Walker. "Mother," he said, "the National Board told us to educate and agitate but not to organize; that was to come later."

"I'm going to organize these men tonight," said I.

"I'm reckoning I'm not going to be mining coal so long in this world and I thought I'd like to die organized," said the spokesman for the group.

I brought the other miners in my room and Mr. Walker gave them the obligation.

"Now, boys, you are twelve in number. That was the number Christ had. I hope that among your twelve there will be no Judas, no one who will betray his fellow. The work you do is for your children and for the future. You preach the gospel of better food, better homes, a decent compensation for the wealth you produce. It is these things that make a great nation."

The spokesman kept up his terrible coughing. He had miner's consumption. As they had no money to pay for their charter I told them that I would attend to that.

Three weeks afterward I had a letter from one of the group. He told me that their spokesman was dead but they had organized eight hundred men and they sent me the money for the charter.

In Caperton Mountain camp I met Duncan Kennedy, who is now commissioner for the mine owners. He and his noble wife gave us shelter and fed us when it was too late for us to go down the mountain and cross the river to an inn. Often after meetings in this mountain district, we sat through the night on the river bank. Frequently we would hear bullets whizz past us as we sat huddled between boulders, our black clothes making us invisible in the blackness of the night.

Seven organizers were sent into Laurel Creek. All came back, shot at, beaten up, run out of town.

One organizer was chased out of town with a gun.

"What did you do?" I said.

"I ran."

"Which way?" said I.

"Mother," he said, "you mustn't go up there. They've got gunmen patrolling the roads."

"That means the miners up there are prisoners," said I, "and need me."

A week later, one Saturday night I went with eight or ten trapper boys to Thayer, a camp about six miles from Laurel Creek. Very early Sunday morning we walked to Laurel Creek. I climbed the mountain so that I could look down on the camp with its huddle of dirty shacks. I sat down on a rock above the camp and told the trapper boys to go down to the town and tell the boys to come up the mountain side. That Mother Jones was going to speak at two o'clock and tell the superintendent that Mother Jones extends a cordial invitation to him to come.

Then I sent two boys across a little gully to a log cabin to get a cup of tea for me. The miner came out and beckoned to me to come over. I went and as I entered the door, my eyes rested on a straw mattress on which rested a beautiful young girl. She looked at me with the most gentle eyes I ever saw in a human being. The wind came in through the cracks of the floor and would raise the bed clothes a little.

I said to the father, "What is wrong with your girl?"

"Consumption," said he. "I couldn't earn enough in the mines and she went to work in a boarding house. They worked her so hard she took sick—consumption."

Around a fireplace sat a group of dirty children, ragged and neglected-looking. He gave us tea and bread.

A great crowd came up the mountain side that afternoon. The superintendent sent one of his lackeys, a colored fellow. When the miners told me who he was and that he was sent there as a spy, I said to him, "See here, young man, don't you know that the immortal Lincoln, a white man, gave you freedom from slavery. Why do you now betray your white brothers who are fighting for industrial freedom?"

"Mother," said he, "I can't make myself scarce but my hearing and my eyesight ain't extra today."

That afternoon, up there on the mountain side, we organized a strong union.

The next day the man who gave me food—his name was Mike Harrington—went to the mines to go to work, but he was told to go to the office and get his pay. No man could work in the mines, the superintendent said, who entertained agitators in his home.

Mike said to him, "I didn't entertain her. She paid me for the tea and bread."

"It makes no difference," said he, "you had Mother Jones in your house and that is sufficient."

He went home and when he opened the door, his sick daughter said, "Father, you have lost your job." She started to sob. That brought on a coughing fit from which she fell back on the pillow exhausted—dead.

That afternoon he was ordered to leave his house as it was owned by the company. They buried the girl and moved to an old barn.

Mike was later made an organizer for the United Mine Workers and he made one of the most faithful workers I have ever known.

In February of 1903, I went to Stanford Mountain where the men were on strike. The court had issued an injunction forbidding the miners from going near the mines. A group of miners walked along the public road nowhere near the mines. The next morning they held a meeting in their own hall which they themselves had built. A United States deputy marshal came into the meeting with warrants for thirty members for violating the injunction.

The men said, "We did not break any law. We did not go near the mines and you know it. We were on the public road."

"Well," said the deputy, "we are going to arrest you anyway."

They defied him to arrest them, insisting they had not violated the law. They gave him twenty-five minutes to leave town. They sent for his brother, who was the company doctor, and told him to take him out.

That night I went to hold a meeting with them. They told me what had happened.

I said, "Boys, it would have been better if you had surrendered, especially as you had the truth on your side and you had not been near the mines."

After the meeting I went to a nearby camp —Montgomery—where there was a little hotel and the railway station. Before leaving, the boys, who came to the edge of the town with me said, "You will be coming back soon, Mother?"

I had no idea how soon it would be.

The next morning I went to the station to get an early train. The agent said to me, "Did you hear what trouble they had up in Stanford Mountain last night?"

"I think you are mistaken," I answered, "for I just came down from there myself last night."

"Well," he said, "they have had some trouble there, all the same."

"Anyone hurt?"

"Yes; I was taking the railway messages and couldn't get all the details. Some shooting."

I said, "Take back my ticket. I must go up to those boys."

I took the short trail up the hillside to Stanford Mountain. It seemed to me as I came toward the camp as if those wretched shacks were huddling closer in terror. Everything was deathly still. As I came nearer the miners' homes, I could hear sobbing. Then I saw between the stilts that propped up a miner's shack the clay red with blood. I pushed open the door. On a mattress, wet with blood, lay a miner. His brains had been blown out while he slept. His shack was riddled with bullets.

In five other shacks men lay dead. In one of them a baby boy and his mother sobbed over the father's corpse. When the little fellow saw me, he said, "Mother Jones, bring back my papa to me. I want to kiss him."

The coroner came. He found that these six men had been murdered in their beds while they peacefully slept; shot by gunmen in the employ of the coal company.

The coroner went. The men were buried on the mountain side. And nothing was ever done to punish the men who had taken their lives.

CHAPTER X

The March of the Mill Children

In the spring of 1903 I went to Kensington, Pennsylvania, where seventy-five thousand textile workers were on strike. Of this number at least ten thousand were little children. The workers were striking for more pay and shorter hours. Every day little children came into Union Headquarters, some with their hands off, some with the thumb missing, some with their fingers off at the knuckle. They were stooped little things, round shouldered and skinny. Many of them were not over ten years of age, although the state law prohibited their working before they were twelve years of age.

The law was poorly enforced and the mothers of these children often swore falsely as to their children's age. In a single block in Kensington, fourteen women, mothers of twenty-two children all under twelve, explained it was a question of starvation or perjury. That the fathers had been killed or maimed at the mines.

I asked the newspaper men why they didn't publish the facts about child labor in Pennsylvania. They said they couldn't because the mill owners had stock in the papers.

"Well, I've got stock in these little children,"

said I, "and I'll arrange a little publicity."

We assembled a number of boys and girls one morning in Independence Park and from there we arranged to parade with banners to the court house where we would hold a meeting.

A great crowd gathered in the public square in front of the city hall. I put the little boys with their fingers off and hands crushed and maimed on a platform. I held up their mutilated hands and showed them to the crowd and made the statement that Philadelphia's mansions were built on the broken bones, the quivering hearts and drooping heads of these children. That their little lives went out to make wealth for others. That neither state or city officials paid any attention to these wrongs. That they did not care that these children were to be the future citizens of the nation.

The officials of the city hall were standing in the open windows. I held the little ones of the mills high up above the heads of the crowd and pointed to their puny arms and legs and hollow chests. They were light to lift.

I called upon the millionaire manufacturers to cease their moral murders, and I cried to the officials in the open windows opposite, "Some day the workers will take possession of your city hall, and when we do, no child will be sacrificed on the altar of profit."

The officials quickly closed the windows, just as they had closed their eyes and hearts.

The reporters quoted my statement that Philadelphia mansions were built on the broken bones and quivering hearts of children. The Philadelphia papers and the New York papers got into a squabble with each other over the question. The universities discussed it. Preachers began talking. That was what I wanted. Public attention on the subject of child labor.

The matter quieted down for a while and I concluded the people needed stirring up again. The Liberty Bell that a century ago rang out for freedom against tyranny was touring the country and crowds were coming to see it everywhere. That gave me an idea. These little children were striking for some of the freedom that childhood ought to have, and I decided that the children and I would go on a tour.

I asked some of the parents if they would let me have their little boys and girls for a week or ten days, promising to bring them back safe and sound. They consented. A man named Sweeny was marshal for our "army." A few men and women went with me to help with the children. They were on strike and I thought they might as well have a little recreation.

The children carried knapsacks on their backs in which was a knife and fork, a tin cup and plate. We took along a wash boiler in which to cook the food on the road. One little fellow had a drum and another had a fife. That was our band. We carried banners that said, "We want

more schools and less hospitals." "We want
time to play." "Prosperity is here. Where is
ours?"

We started from Philadelphia where we held
a great mass meeting. I decided to go with the
children to see President Roosevelt to ask him
to have Congress pass a law prohibiting the exploitation of childhood. I thought that President Roosevelt might see these mill children and
compare them with his own little ones who were
spending the summer on the seashore at Oyster
Bay. I thought, too, out of politeness, we might
call on Morgan in Wall Street who owned the
mines where many of these children's fathers
worked.

The children were very happy, having plenty
to eat, taking baths in the brooks and rivers
every day. I thought when the strike is over
and they go back to the mills, they will never
have another holiday like this. All along the
line of march the farmers drove out to meet us
with wagon loads of fruit and vegetables. Their
wives brought the children clothes and money.
The interurban trainmen would stop their
trains and give us free rides.

Marshal Sweeny and I would go ahead to the
towns and arrange sleeping quarters for the
children, and secure meeting halls. As we
marched on, it grew terribly hot. There was no
rain and the roads were heavy with dust. From
time to time we had to send some of the children

back to their homes. They were too weak to stand the march.

We were on the outskirts of New Trenton, New Jersey, cooking our lunch in the wash boiler, when the conductor on the interurban car stopped and told us the police were coming down to notify us that we could not enter the town. There were mills in the town and the mill owners didn't like our coming.

I said, "All right, the police will be just in time for lunch."

Sure enough, the police came and we invited them to dine with us. They looked at the little gathering of children with their tin plates and cups around the wash boiler. They just smiled and spoke kindly to the children, and said nothing at all about not going into the city.

We went in, held our meeting, and it was the wives of the police who took the little children and cared for them that night, sending them back in the morning with a nice lunch rolled up in paper napkins.

Everywhere we had meetings, showing up with living children, the horrors of child labor.

At one town the mayor said we could not hold a meeting because he did not have sufficient police protection. "These little children have never known any sort of protection, your honor," I said, "and they are used to going without it." He let us have our meeting.

One night in Princeton, New Jersey, we slept

in the big cool barn on Grover Cleveland's great estate. The heat became intense. There was much suffering in our ranks, for our little ones were not robust. The proprietor of the leading hotel sent for me. "Mother," he said, "order what you want and all you want for your army, and there's nothing to pay."

I called on the mayor of Princeton and asked for permission to speak opposite the campus of the University. I said I wanted to speak on higher education. The mayor gave me permission. A great crowd gathered, professors and students and the people; and I told them that the rich robbed these little children of any education of the lowest order that they might send their sons and daughters to places of higher education. That they used the hands and feet of little children that they might buy automobiles for their wives and police dogs for their daughters to talk French to. I said the mill owners take babies almost from the cradle. And I showed those professors children in our army who could scarcely read or write because they were working ten hours a day in the silk mills of Pennsylvania.

"Here's a text book on economics," I said, pointing to a little chap, James Ashworth, who was ten years old and who was stooped over like an old man from carrying bundles of yarn that weighed seventy-five pounds. "He gets three dollars a week and his sister who is fourteen gets six dollars. They work in a carpet factory ten hours a day while the children of the rich are getting their higher education.''

That night we camped on the banks of Stony Brook where years and years before the ragged Revolutionary Army camped, Washington's brave soldiers that made their fight for freedom.

From Jersey City we marched to Hoboken. I sent a committee over to the New York Chief of Police, Ebstein, asking for permission to march up Fourth Avenue to Madison Square where I wanted to hold a meeting. The chief refused and forbade our entrance to the city.

I went over myself to New York and saw Mayor Seth Low. The mayor was most courteous but he said he would have to support the police commissioner. I asked him what the reason was for refusing us entrance to the city and he said that we were not citizens of New York.

''Oh, I think we will clear that up, Mr. Mayor,'' I said. ''Permit me to call your attention to an incident which took place in this nation just a year ago. A piece of rotten royalty came over here from Germany, called Prince Henry. The Congress of the United States voted $45,000 to fill that fellow's stomach for three weeks and to entertain him. His brother was getting $4,000,000 dividends out of the blood of the workers in this country. Was he a citizen of this land?"

"And it was reported, Mr. Mayor, that you and all the officials of New York and the University Club entertained that chap." And I repeated, "Was he a citizen of New York?"

"No, Mother," said the mayor, "he was not."

"And a Chinaman called Lee Woo was also entertained by the officials of New York. Was he a citizen of New York?"

"No, Mother, he was not."

"Did they ever create any wealth for our nation?"

"No, Mother, they did not," said he.

"Well, Mr. Mayor, these are the little citizens of the nation and they also produce its wealth. Aren't we entitled to enter your city?"

"Just wait," says he, and he called the commissioner of police over to his office.

Well, finally they decided to let the army come in. We marched up Fourth Avenue to Madison Square and police officers, captains, sergeants, roundsmen and reserves from three precincts accompanied us. But the police would not let us hold a meeting in Madison Square. They insisted that the meeting be held in Twentieth Street.

I pointed out to the captain that the single taxers were allowed to hold meetings in the square. "Yes," he said, "but they won't have twenty people and you might have twenty thousand.''

We marched to Twentieth Street. I told an immense crowd of the horrors of child labor in the mills around the anthracite region and I showed them some of the children. I showed them Eddie Dunphy, a little fellow of twelve, whose job it was to sit all day on a high stool, handing in the right thread to another worker. Eleven hours a day he sat on the high stool with dangerous machinery all about him. All day long, winter and summer, spring and fall, for three dollars a week.

And then I showed them Gussie Rangnew, a little girl from whom all the childhood had gone. Her face was like an old woman's. Gussie packed stockings in a factory, eleven hours a day for a few cents a day.

We raised a lot of money for the strikers and hundreds of friends offered their homes to the little ones while we were in the city.

The next day we went to Coney Island at the invitation of Mr. Bostick who owned the wild animal show. The children had a wonderful day such as they never had in all their lives. After the exhibition of the trained animals, Mr. Bostick let me speak to the audience. There was a back drop to the tiny stage of the Roman Colosseum with the audience painted in and two Roman emperors down in front with their thumbs down. Right in front of the emperors were the empty iron cages of the animals. I put my little children in the cages and they clung to the iron bars while I talked.

I told the crowd that the scene was typical of the aristocracy of employers with their thumbs down to the little ones of the mills and factories, and people sitting dumbly by.

"We want President Roosevelt to hear the wail of the children who never have a chance to go to school but work eleven and twelve hours a day in the textile mills of Pennsylvania; who weave the carpets that he and you walk upon; and the lace curtains in your windows, and the clothes of the people. Fifty years ago there was a cry against slavery and men gave up their lives to stop the selling of black children on the block. Today the white child is sold for two dollars a week to the manufacturers. Fifty years ago the black babies were sold C. O. D. Today the white baby is sold on the installment plan.

"In Georgia where children work day and night in the cotton mills they have just passed a bill to protect song birds. What about the little children from whom all song is gone?

"I shall ask the president in the name of the aching hearts of these little ones that he emancipate them from slavery. I will tell the president that the prosperity he boasts of is the prosperity of the rich wrung from the poor and the helpless.

"The trouble is that no one in Washington cares. I saw our legislators in one hour pass three bills for the relief of the railways but when labor cries for aid for the children they will not listen.

"I asked a man in prison once how he happened to be there and he said he had stolen a pair of shoes. I told him if he had stolen a railroad he would be a United States Senator.

"We are told that every American boy has the chance of being president. I tell you that these little boys in the iron cages would sell their chance any day for good square meals and a chance to play. These little toilers whom I have taken from the mills—deformed, dwarfed in body and soul, with nothing but toil before them—have never heard that they have a chance, the chance of every American male citizen, to become the president.

"You see those monkeys in those cages over there." I pointed to a side cage. "The professors are trying to teach them to talk. The monkeys are too wise for they fear that the manufacturers would buy them for slaves in their factories."

I saw a stylishly dressed young man down in the front of the audience. Several times he grinned. I stopped speaking and pointing to him I said, 'Stop your smiling, young man! Leave this place! Go home and beg the mother who bore you in pain, as the mothers of these

n, go home and beg her
d a heart.''

out, followed by the eyes
the cage. The people sat
it in the rear a lion roared.

we left Coney Island for Man-
to visit Senator Platt, who had
made   pointment to see me at nine o'clock
in the morning. The children got stuck in the
sand banks and I had a time cleaning the sand
off the littlest ones. So we started to walk on
the railroad track. I was told it was private
property and we had to get off. Finally a
saloon keeper showed us a short cut into the
sacred grounds of the hotel and suddenly the
armp appeared in the lobby. The little fellows
played ''Hail, hail, the gang's all here'' on
their fifes and drums, and Senator Platt when
he saw the little army ran away through the
back door to New York.

I asked the manager if he would give the
children breakfast and charge it up to the
Senator as we had an invitation to breakfast
that morning with him. He gave us a private
room and he gave those children such a breakfast as they had never had in all their lives.
I had breakfast too, and a reporter from one
of the Hearst papers and I charged it all up
to Senator Platt.

We marched down to Oyster Bay but the
president refused to see us and he would not

answer my letters. But our march had done its work. We had drawn the attention of the nation to the crime of child labor. And while the strike of the textile workers in Kensington was lost and the children driven back to work, not long afterward the Pennsylvania legislature passed a child labor law that sent thousands of children home from the mills, and kept thousands of others from entering the factory until they were fourteen years of age.

CHAPTER XI

THOSE MULES WON'T SCAB TODAY

Lattimer was an eye-sore to the miners. It seemed as if no one could break into it. Twenty-six organizers and union men had been killed in that coal camp in previous strikes. Some of them had been shot in the back. The blood of union men watered the highways. No one dared go in.

I said nothing about it but made up my mind that I was going there some night. After the raid of the women in Coaldale in the Panther Creek, the general manager of Lattimer said that if I came in there I would go out a corpse. I made no reply but I set my plans and I did not consult an undertaker.

From three different camps in the Panther Creek I had a leader bring a group of strikers to a junction of the road that leads into Lattimer. There I met them with my army of women again.

As I was leaving the hotel the clerk said, "Mother, the reporters told me to ring their bell if I saw you go out."

"Well, don't see me go out. Watch the front door carefully and I will go out the back door."

We marched through the night, reaching Lattimer just before dawn. The strikers hid themselves in the mines. The women took up their position on the door steps of the miners' shacks. When a miner stepped out of his house to go to work, the women started mopping the step, shouting, "No work today!"

Everybody came running out into the dirt streets. "God, it is the old mother and her army," they were all saying.

The Lattimer miners and the mule drivers were afraid to quit work. They had been made cowards. They took the mules, lighted the lamps in their caps and started down the mines, not knowing that I had three thousand miners down below ground waiting for them and the mules.

"Those mules won't scab today," I said to the general manager who was cursing everybody. "They know it is going to be a holiday."

"Take those mules down!" shouted the general manager.

Mules and drivers and miners disappeared down into the earth. I kept the women singing patriotic songs so as to drown the noise of the men down in the mines.

Directly the mules came up to the surface without a driver, and we women cheered for the mules who were the first to become good union citizens. They were followed by the miners who began running home. Those that didn't go up were sent up. Those that insisted on working and thus defeating their brothers were grabbed by the women and carried to their wives.

An old Irish woman had two sons who were scabs. The women threw one of them over the fence to his mother. He lay there still. His mother thought he was dead and she ran into the house for a bottle of holy water and shook it over Mike.

"Oh for God's sake, come back to life," she hollered. "Come back and join the union."

He opened his eyes and saw our women standing around him.

"Shure, I'll go to hell before I'll scab again," says he.

The general manager called the sheriff who asked me to take the women away. I said, "Sheriff, no one is going to get hurt, no property is going to be destroyed but there are to be no more killings of innocent men here."

I told him if he wanted peace he should put up a notice that the mines were closed until the strike was settled.

The day was filled with excitement. The deputies kept inside the office; the general manager also. Our men stayed up at the mines to attend to the scabs and the women did the rest. As a matter of fact the majority of the men, those with any spirit left in them after years of cowardice, wanted to strike but had not dared. But when a hand was held out to them, they took hold and marched along with their brothers.

The bosses telephoned to John Mitchell that he should take me and my army of women out of Lattimer. That was the first knowledge that Mitchell had of my being there.

When the manager saw there was no hope and that the battle was won by the miners, he came out and put up a notice that the mines were closed until the strike was settled.

I left Lattimer with my army of women and went up to Hazelton. President Mitchell and his organizers were there. Mr. Mitchell said, "Weren't you afraid to go in there?"

"No," I said, "I am not afraid to face any thing if facing it may bring relief to the class that I belong to."

The victory of Lattimer gave new life to the whole anthracite district. It gave courage to the organization. Those brave women I shall never forget who caused those stone walls to fall by marching around with tin pans and cat calls.

Soon afterward, a convention was called and the strike was settled. The organizers got up a document asking every miner to subscribe so much to purchase a $10,000 house for John Mitchell. The document happened to come into my hands at the convention which was called to call off the victorious strike. I arose and I said:

"If John Mitchell can't buy a house to suit him for his wife and for his family out of his salary, then I would suggest that he get a job that will give him a salary to buy a $10,000 house. Most of you do not own a shingle on the roof that covers you. Every decent man buys a house for his own wife first before he buys a house for another man's wife.

I was holding the petition as I spoke and I tore it up and threw the bits on the floor. " 'Tis you men and your women who won the strike," I said, "with your sacrifice and your patience and your forbearance through all these past weary months. 'Tis the sacrifice of your brothers in other trades who sent the strike benefits week in and week out that enabled you to make the fight to the end."

From then on Mitchell was not friendly to me. He took my attitude as one of personal enmity. And he saw that he could not control me. He had tasted power and this finally destroyed him. I believe that no man who holds a leader's position should ever accept favors from either side. He is then committed to show favors. A leader must stand alone.

CHAPTER XII

How the Women Mopped Up Coaldale

In Lonaconia, Maryland, there was a strike. I was there. In Hazelton, Pennsylvania, a convention was called to discuss the anthracite strike. I was there when they issued the strike call. One hundred and fifty thousand men responded. The men of Scranton and Shamokin and Coaldale and Panther Creek and Valley Battle. And I was there.

In Shamokin I met Miles Daugherty, an organizer. When he quit work and drew his pay, he gave one-half of his pay envelope to his wife and the other half he kept to rent halls and pay for lights for the union. Organizers did not draw much salary in those days and they did heroic, unselfish work.

Not far from Shamokin, in a little mountain town, the priest was holding a meeting when I went in. He was speaking in the church. I spoke in an open field. The priest told the men to go back and obey their masters and their reward would be in Heaven. He denounced the strikers as children of darkness. The miners left the church in a body and marched over to my meeting.

"Boys," I said, "this strike is called in order that you and your wives and your little ones may get a bit of Heaven before you die."

We organized the entire camp.

The fight went on. In Coaldale, in the Hazelton district, the miners were not permitted to assemble in any hall. It was necessary to win the strike in that district that the Coaldale miners be organized.

I went to a nearby mining town that was thoroughly organized and asked the women if they would help me get the Coaldale men out. This was in McAdoo. I told them to leave their men at home to take care of the family. I asked them to put on their kitchen clothes and bring mops and brooms with them and a couple of tin pans. We marched over the mountains fifteen miles, beating on the tin pans as if they were cymbals. At three o'clock in the morning we met the Crack Thirteen of the militia, patroling the roads to Coaldale. The colonel of the regiment said "Halt! Move back!"

I said, "Colonel, the working men of America will not halt nor will they ever go back. The working man is going forward!"

"I'll charge bayonets," said he.

"On whom?"

"On your people."

"We are not enemies," said I. "We are just a band of working women whose brothers and husbands are in a battle for bread. We want

our brothers in Coaldale to join us in our fight.
We are here on the mountain road for our children's sake, for the nation's sake. We are not
going to hurt anyone and surely you would not
hurt us.''

They kept us there till daybreak and when
they saw the army of women in kitchen aprons,
with dishpans and mops, they laughed and let
us pass. An army of strong mining women
makes a wonderfully spectacular picture.

Well, when the miners in the Coaldale camp
started to go to work they were met by the
McAdoo women who were beating on their pans
and shouting, ''Join the union! Join the
union!''

They joined, every last man of them, and we
got so enthusiastic that we organized the street
car men who promised to haul no scabs for the
coal companies. As there were no other groups
to organize we marched over the mountains
home, beating on our pans and singing patriotic
songs.

Meanwhile President Mitchell and all his organizers were sleeping in the Valley Hotel over
in Hazelton. They knew nothing of our march
onto Coaldale until the newspaper men telephoned to him that ''Mother Jones was raising
hell up in the mountains with a bunch of wild
women!''

He, of course, got nervous. He might have
gotten more nervous if he had known how we

made the mine bosses go home and how we told
their wives to clean them up and make decent
American citizens out of them. How we went
around to the kitchen of the hotel where the
militia were quartered and ate the breakfast
that was on the table for the soldiers.

When I got back to Hazelton, Mitchell looked
at me with surprise. I was worn out. Coaldale had been a strenous night and morning and
its thirty mile tramp. I assured Mitchell that
no one had been hurt and no property injured.
The military had acted like human beings.
They took the matter as a joke. They enjoyed
the morning's fun. I told him how scared the
sheriff had been. He had been talking to me
without knowing who I was.

"Oh Lord," he said, "that Mother Jones is
sure a dangerous woman."

"Why don't you arrest her?" I asked him.

"Oh Lord, I couldn't I'd have that mob of
women with their mops and brooms after me
and the jail ain't big enough to hold them all.
They'd mop the life out of a fellow!"

Mr. Mitchell said, "My God, Mother, did you
get home safe? What did you do?"

"I got five thousand men out and organized
them. We had time left over so we organized
the street car men and they will not haul any
scabs into camp."

"Did you get hurt, Mother?"

"No, we did the hurting."

"Didn't the superintendents' bosses get after you?"

"No, we got after them. Their wives and our women were yelling around like cats. It was a great fight."

CHAPTER XIII

THE CRIPPLE CREEK STRIKE
(1903)

The state of Colorado belonged not to a republic but to the Colorado Fuel and Iron Company, the Victor Company and their dependencies. The governor was their agent. The militia under Bell did their bidding. Whenever the masters of the state told the governor to bark, he yelped for them like a mad hound. Whenever they told the military to bite, they bit.

The people of Colorado had voted overwhelmingly for an eight-hour day. The legislature passed an eight-hour law but the courts had declared it unconstitutional. Then when the measure was submitted directly to the people, they voted for it with 40,000 votes majority. But the next legislature, which was controlled by the mining interests, failed to pass the bill.

The miners saw that they could not get their demands through peaceful legislation. That they must fight. That they must strike. All the metal miners struck first. The strike extended into New Mexico and Utah. It became an ugly war. The metal miners were anxious to have the coal miners join them in their struggle.

The executive board of the United Mine Workers was in session in Indianapolis and to this board the governor of Colorado had sent a delegation to convince them that there ought not to be a strike in the coal fields. Among the delegates, was a labor commissioner.

I was going on my way to West Virginia from Mount Olive, Illinois, where the miners were commemorating their dead. I stopped off at headquarters in Indianapolis. The executive board asked me to go to Colorado, look into conditions there, see what the sentiments of the miners were, and make a report to the office.

I went immediately to Colorado, first to the office of The Western Federation of Miners where I heard the story of the industrrial conflict. I then got myself an old calico dress, a sunbonnet, some pins and needles, elastic and tape and such sundries, and went down to the southern coal fields of the Colorado Fuel and Iron Company.

As a peddler, I went through the various coal camps, eating in the homes of the miners, staying all night with their families. I found the conditions under which they lived deplorable. They were in practical slavery to the company, who owned their houses, owned all the land, so that if a miner did own a house he must vacate whenever it pleased the land owners. They were paid in scrip instead of money so that they could not go away if dissatisfied. They must buy at company stores and at company prices. The coal they mined was weighed by an agent of the company and the miners could not have a check weighman to see that full credit was given them. The schools, the churches, the roads belonged to the Company. I felt, after listening to their stories, after witnessing their long patience that the time was ripe for revolt against such brutal conditions.

I went to Trinidad and to the office of the Western Federation of Miners. I talked with the secretary, Gillmore, a loyal, hard-working man, and with the President, Howell, a good, honest soul. We sat up and talked the matter over far into the night. I showed them the conditions I had found down in the mining camps were heart-rending, and I felt it was our business to remedy those conditions and bring some future, some sunlight at least into the lives of the children. They deputized me to go at once to headquarters in Indianapolis.

I took the train the next morning. When I arrived at the office in Indianapolis, I found the president, John Mitchell, the vice-president, T. L. Lewis, the secretary, W. B. Wilson of Arnot, Pennsylvania, and a board member, called "old man Ream," from Iowa. These officers told me to return at once to Colorado and they would call a strike of the coal miners.

The strike was called November 9th, 1903. The demand was for an eight hour day, a check weighman representing the miners, payment in money instead of scrip. The whole state of Colorado was in revolt. No coal was dug. November is a cold month in Colorado and the citizens began to feel the pressure of the strike.

Late one evening in the latter part of November I came into the hotel. I had been working all day and into the night among the miners and their families, helping to distribute food and clothes, encouraging, holding meetings. As I was about to retire, the hotel clerk called me down to answer a long distance telephone call from Louisville. The voice said, "Oh for God's sake, Mother, come to us, come to us!"

I asked what the trouble was and the reply was more a cry than an answer, "Oh don't wait to ask. Don't miss the train."

I got Mr. Howell, the president, on the telephone and asked him what was the trouble in Louisville.

"They are having a convention there," he said.

"A convention, is it, and what for?"

"To call off the strike in the northern coal fields because the operators have yielded to the demands." He did not look at me as he spoke. I could see he was heart sick.

"But they cannot go back until the operators settle with the southern miners," I said. "They will not desert their brothers until the strike is won! Are you going to let them do it?"

"Oh Mother," he almost cried, "I can't help it. It is the National Headquarters who have ordered them back!"

"That's treachery," I said, "quick, get ready and come with me."

We telephoned down to the station to have the conductor hold the train for Louisville a few minutes. This he did. We got into Louisville the next morning. I had not slept. The board member, Ream, and Grant Hamilton, representing the Federation of Labor, came to the hotel where I was stopping and asked where Mr. Howell, the president was.

"He has just stepped out," I said. "He will be back."

"Well, meantime, I want to notify you," Ream said, "that you must not block the settlement of the northern miners because the National President, John Mitchell, wants it, and he pays you."

"Are you through?" said I.

He nodded.

"Then I am going to tell you that if God Almighty wants this strike called off for his benefit and not for the miners, I am going to raise my voice against it. And as to President John paying me . . . he never paid me a

penny in his life. It is the hard earned nickels
and dimes of the miners that pay me, and it is
their interests that I am going to serve.''

I went to the convention and heard the matter of the northern miners returning to the
mines discussed. I watched two shrewd diplo-
mats deal with unsophisticated men; Struby,
the president of the northern coal fields, and
Blood, one of the keenest, trickiest lawyers in
the West. And behind them, John Mitchell,
toasted and wined and dined, flattered and ca-
joled by the Denver Citizens' Alliance, and the
Civic Federation was pulling the strings.

In the afternoon the miners called on me to
address the convention.

"Brothers," I said, "You English speaking
miners of the northern fields promised your
southern brothers, seventy per cent of whom
do not speak English, that you would support
them to the end. Now you are asked to betray
them, to make a separate settlement. You
have a common enemy and it is your duty
to fight to a finish. The enemy seeks to
conquer by dividing your ranks, by making
distinctions between North and South, between
American and foreign. You are all miners,
fighting a common cause, a common master.
The iron heel feels the same to all flesh.
Hunger and suffering and the cause of
your children bind more closely than a
common tongue. I am accused of helping

the Western Federation of Miners, as if
that were a crime, by one of the National
board members. I plead guilty. I know no
East or West, North nor South when it comes
to my class fighting the battle for justice. If it
is my fortune to live to see the industrial chain
broken from every workingman's child in
America, and if then there is one black child in
Africa in bondage, there shall I go."

The delegates rose en masse to cheer. The
vote was taken. The majority decided to stand
by the southern miners, refusing to obey the
national President.

The Denver Post reported my speech and a
copy was sent to Mr. Mitchell in Indianapolis.
He took the paper in to his secretary and said,
pointing to the report, "See what Mother Jones
has done to me!"

Three times Mitchell tried to make the northern miners return to the mines but each time he
was unsuccessful. "Mitchell has got to get
Mother Jones out of the field," an organizer
said. "He can never lick the Federation as
long as she is in there."

I was informed that Mitchell went to the governor and asked him to put me out of the state.

Finally the ultimatum was given to the
northern miners. All support for the strike
was withdrawn. The northern miners accepted
the operators' terms and returned to work.
Their act created practical peonage in the south

and the strike was eventually lost, although the struggle in the south went on for a year.

Much of the fighting took place around Cripple Creek. The miners were evicted from their company-owned houses. They went out on the bleak mountain sides, lived in tents through a terrible winter with the temperature below zero, with eighteen inches of snow on the ground. They tied their feet in gunny sacks and lived lean and lank and hungry as timber wolves. They received sixty-three cents a week strike benefit while John Mitchell went traveling through Europe, staying at fashionable hotels, studying the labor movement. When he returned the miners had been lashed back into the mines by hunger but John Mitchell was given a banquet in the Park Avenue Hotel and presented with a watch with diamonds.

From the day I opposed John Mitchell's authority, the guns were turned on me. Slander and persecution followed me like black shadows. But the fight went on.

One night when I came in from the field where I had been holding meetings, I was just dropping to sleep when a knock—a loud knock —came on my door. I always slept in my clothes for I never knew what might happen. I went to the door, opened it, and faced a military chap.

"The Colonel wants you up at headquarters."

I went with him immediately. Three or four others were brought in: War John and Joe Pajammy, organizers. We were all taken down to the Santa Fe station. While standing there, waiting for the train that was to deport us, some of the miners ran down to bid me good-bye. "Mother, good-bye," they said, stretching out their hands to take mine.

The colonel struck their hands and yelled at them. "Get away from there. You can't shake hands with that woman!"

The militia took us to La Junta. They handed me a letter from the governor, notifying me that under no circumstances could I return to the State of Colorado. I sat all night in the station. In the morning the Denver train came along. I had no food, no money. I asked the conductor to take me to Denver. He said he would.

"Well," I said, "I don't want you to lose your job."

I showed him the letter from the governor. He read it.

"Mother," he said, "do you want to go to Denver?"

"I do," said I.

"Then to Hell with the job;" said he, "it's to Denver you go."

In Denver I got a room and rested a while. I sat down and wrote a letter to the governor, the obedient little boy of the coal companies.

"Mr. Governor, you notified your dogs of war to put me out of the state. They complied with your instructions. I hold in my hand a letter that was handed to me by one of them, which says 'under no circumstances return to this state.' I wish to notify you, governor, that you don't own the state. When it was admitted to the sisterhood of states, my fathers gave me a share of stock in it; and that is all they gave to you. The civil courts are open. If I break a law of state or nation it is the duty of the civil courts to deal with me. That is why my forefathers established those courts to keep dictators and tyrants such as you from interfering with civilians. I am right here in the capital, after being out nine or ten hours, four or five blocks from your office. I want to ask you, governor, what in Hell are you going to do about it?"

I called a messenger and sent it up to the governor's office. He read it and a reporter who was present in the office at the time told me his face grew red.

"What shall I do?" he said to the reporter. He was used to acting under orders.

"Leave her alone," counselled the reporter. "There is no more patriotic citizen in America."

From Denver I went down the Western Slope, holding meetings, cheering and encouraging those toiling and disinherited miners who were fighting against such monstrous odds.

I went to Helper, Utah, and got a room with a very nice Italian family. I was to hold a meeting Sunday afternoon. From every quarter the men came, trudging miles over the mountains. The shop men were notified not to come but they came anyhow. Just as the meeting was about to open, the mayor of the little town came to me and said that I could not hold a meeting; that I was on company ground. I asked him how far his jurisdiction extended. He said as far as the Company's jurisdiction. He was a Company mayor.

So I turned to the audience and asked them to follow me. The audience to a man followed me to a little tent colony at Half Way that the miners had established when they had been evicted from their homes.

When the meeting closed I returned to Helper. The next day, although there was no smallpox in town, a frame shack was built to isolate smallpox sufferers in. I was notified that I had been exposed to smallpox and must be incarcerated in the shack. But somehow that night the shack burned down.

I went to stay in Half Way because the Italian family were afraid to keep me longer. Another Italian family gave me a bare room in their shack. There was only a big stone to fasten the door. No sooner was I located than the militia notified me that I was in quarantine because I had been exposed to smallpox. But I used to go out and talk to the miners and they used to come to me.

One Saturday night I got tipped off by the postoffice master that the militia were going to raid the little tent colony in the early morning. I called the miners to me and asked them if they had guns. Sure, they had guns. They were western men, men of the mountains. I told them to go bury them between the boulders; deputies were coming to take them away from them. I did not tell them that there was to be a raid for I did not want any bloodshed. Better to submit to arrest.

Between 4:30 and 5 o'clock in the morning I heard the tramp of feet on the road. I looked out of my smallpox window and saw about forty-five deputies. They descended upon the sleeping tent colony, dragged the miners out of their beds. They did not allow them to put on their clothing. The miners begged to be allowed to put on their clothes, for at that early hour the mountain range is the coldest. Shaking with cold, followed by the shrieks and wails of their wives and children, beaten along the road by guns, they were driven like cattle to Helper. In the evening they were packed in a box car and run down to Price, the county seat and put in jail.

Not one law had these miners broken. The pitiful screams of the women and children would have penetrated Heaven. Their tears melted the heart of the Mother of Sorrows. Their crime was that they had struck against the power of gold.

The women huddled beneath the window of the house where I was incarcerated for small-pox.

"Oh Mother, what shall we do?" they wailed. "What's to become of our little children!"

"See my little Johnny," said one woman, holding up a tiny, red baby—new born.

"That's a nice baby," I said.

"He sick. Pretty soon he die. Company take house. Company take my man. Pretty soon company take my baby."

Two days after this raid was made, the stone that held my door was suddenly pushed in. A fellow jumped into the room, stuck a gun under my jaw and told me to tell him where he could get $3,000 of the miners' money or he would blow out my brains.

"Don't waste your powder," I said. "You write the miners up in Indianapolis. Write Mitchell. He's got money now."

"I don't want any of your damn talk," he replied, then asked:

"Hasn't the president got money?"

"You got him in jail."

"Haven't you got any money?"

"Sure!" I put my hand in my pocket, took out fifty cents and turned the pocket inside out.

"Is that all you got?"

"Sure, and I'm not going to give it to you, for I want it to get a jag on to boil the Helen Gould smallpox out of my system so I will not inoculate the whole nation when I get out of here."

"How are you going to get out of here if you haven't money when they turn you loose?"

"The railway men will take me anywhere."

There were two other deputies outside. They kept hollering for him to come out. "She ain't got any money," they kept insisting. Finally he was convinced that I had nothing.

This man, I afterward found out, had been a bank robber, but had been sworn in as deputy to crush the miners' union. He was later killed while robbing the post office in Prince. Yet he was the sort of man who was hired by the moneyed interests to crush the hopes and aspirations of the fathers and mothers and even the children of the workers.

I was held twenty-six days and nights in that bare room, isolated for smallpox. Finally with no redress I was turned loose and went to Salt Lake. During all those days and nights I did not undress because of imminent danger.

All civil law had broken down in the Cripple Creek strike. The militia under Colonel Verdeckberg said, "We are under orders only from God and Governor Peabody." Judge Advocate McClelland when accused of violating the con-

stitution said, "To hell with the constitution!"
There was a complete breakdown of all civil
law. Habeas corpus proceedings were suspended. Free speech and assembly were forbidden.
People spoke in whispers as in the days of the
inquisition. Soldiers committed outrages.
Strikers were arrested for vagrancy and
worked in chain gangs on the street under
brutal soldiers. Men, women and tiny children
were packed in the Bullpen at Cripple Creek.
Miners were shot dead as they slept. They
were ridden from the country, their families
knowing not where they had gone, or whether
they lived.

When the strike started in Cripple Creek, the
civil law was operating, but the governor, a
banker, and in complete sympathy with the
Rockefeller interests, sent the militia. They
threw the officers out of office. Sheriff Robin-
son had a rope thrown at his feet and told that
if he did not resign, the rope would be about
his neck.

Three men were brought into Judge Seeds'
court—miners. There was no charge lodged
against them. He ordered them released but
the soldiers who with drawn bayonets had attended the hearing, immediately rearrested
them and took them back to jail.

Four hundred men were taken from their
homes. Seventy-six of these were placed on a
train, escorted to Kansas, dumped out on a

prairie and told never to come back, except to meet death.

In the heat of June, in Victor, 1600 men were arrested and put in the Armory Hall. Bull-pens were established and anyone be he miner, or a woman or a child that incurred the displeasure of the great coal interests, or the militia, were thrown into these horrible stockades.

Shop keepers were forbidden to sell to miners. Priests and ministers were intimidated, fearing to give them consolation. The miners opened their own stores to feed the women and children. The soldiers and hoodlums broke into the stores, looted them, broke open the safes, destroyed the scales, ripped open the sacks of flour and sugar, dumped them on the floor and poured kerosene oil over everything. The beef and meat was poisoned by the militia. Goods were stolen. The miners were without redress, for the militia was immune.

And why were these things done? Because a group of men had demanded an eight hour day, a check weighman and the abolition of the scrip system that kept them in serfdom to the mighty coal barons. That was all. Just that miners had refused to labor under these conditions. Just because miners wanted a better chance for their children, more of the sunlight, more freedom. And for this they suffered one whole year and for this they died.

Perhaps no one in the labor movement has seen more brutality perpetrated upon the workers than I have seen. I have seen them killed in industry, worn out and made old before their time, jailed and shot if they protested. Story after story I could tell of persecution and of bravery unequalled on any battle field .

There was Mrs. M. F. Langdon of Cripple Creek. ''The Victor Record,'' a newspaper giving the miners' side of the strike, had been arbitrarily suppressed by the militia, as were all journals that did not espouse the cause of the coal operators. Her husband had been arrested because he was the editor of The Record.

The military were surprised when the morning after the suppression of the paper and the jailing of the editor and his helpers, the paper came out as usual. Throughout the night Mrs. Langdon, working with a tiny candle, had set the type and run the sheets out on a hand press.

On November 19, 1903, two organizers, Demolli and Price, were going to Scofield when a short distance from town, a mob composed of members of the ''citizens' alliance'' boarded the train armed with high-powered rifles, and ordered the train crew to take the organizers back.

In December, Lucianno Desentos and Joseph Vilano were killed outright by deputy sheriffs at Secundo. Soon after their killing, the home

of William G. Isaac, an organizer, was blown
up. He was in Glenwood Springs when it
occurred. Part of the house was wrecked by the
explosion, the part in which his two little children usually slept. The night of the explosion,
however, they slept in the back room with their
mother. The family was saved from being
burned to death in the fire that followed the explosion by crawling through a broken window.
Isaac was arrested and charged with attempt-
ing the murder of his wife and children.

And so I could go on and on. Men beaten
and left for dead in the road. The home of
Sherman Parker searched without warrants, his
wife in her nightclothes made to hold the light
for the soldiers. And no arms found.

On Sunday in February of 1914, Joe Panonia
and myself went to a camp out in Berwyn to
hold a meeting, and William Farley and James
Mooney, national organizers, went to Bohnn.
Both settlements lay in the same direction,
Berwyn being a little further on. As we drove
through Bohnn after our meeting, three women
ran out from a shack, waving their long, bony
arms at us and shrieking and whirling around
like witches. They jumped right in front of
our automobile in the narrow road.

"Come in! Come in! Something bad!"
They put their hands to their heads and rocked
sidewise. They were foreigners and knew
little English.

"Joe," I said, "we'd better drive on. They may have been drinking. It may be some sort of hoax to get us into the house."

"No! No!" shrieked the women. "No drink! Something bad!" They climbed on the running board and began pulling us.

"Come on, Mother," said Joe. "Let's go in. I think there has been trouble."

We followed the three lanky women into the shack. On a wretched bed covered with dirty rag-ends of blankets and old quilts lay Mooney, bleeding profusely and unconscious. Farley sat beside him, badly beaten.

Joe raced into Trinidad and got a doctor but although Mooney survived he was never quite right in the head afterward. Farley, however, recovered from his terrible beating.

He said that as they were returning from Bohhn, seven gunmen jumped out from the bushes along the road, had beaten them up, kicked them and stamped their feet upon them. All seven were armed and resistance was useless.

Organizers were thrown into jail and held without trial for months. They were deported. In April fourteen miners were arrested at Broadhead and deported to New Mexico. They were landed in the desert, thirty miles from food or water. Hundreds of others were deported, taken away without being allowed to communicate with wives and children. The women suffered agonies not knowing when their men went from home whether they would ever return. If the deported men returned they were immediately arrested by the militia and put in jail. All organizers and leaders were in danger of death, in the open streets or from ambush. John Lawson was shot at but by a miracle the bullet missed him.

The strike in the southern fields dragged on and on. But from the moment the southern miners had been deserted by their northern brothers, I felt their strike was doomed. Bravely did those miners fight before giving in to the old peonage. The military had no regard for human life. They were sanctified cannibals. Is it any wonder that we have murders and holdups when the youth of the land is trained by the great industrialists to a belief in force; when they see that the possession of money puts one above law.

Men like President Howell and Secretary Simpson will live in history. I was in close touch with them throughout this terrible strike. Their descendants should feel proud that the blood of such great men flows in their veins.

No more loyal, courageous men could be found than those southern miners, scornfully referred to by "citizens' alliances" as "foreigners." Italians and Mexicans endured to the end. They were defeated on the industrial field but theirs was the victory of the spirit.

CHAPTER XIV

CHILD LABOR

I have always advised men to read. All my life I have told them to study the works of those great authors who have been interested in making this world a happier place for those who do its drudgery. When there were no strikes, I held educational meetings and after the meetings I would sell the book, "Merrie England," which told in simple fashion of the workers' struggle for a more abundant life.

"Boys," I would say, "listen to me. Instead of going to the pool and gambling rooms, go up to the mountain and read this book. Sit under the trees, listen to the birds and take a lesson from those little feathered creatures who do not exploit one another, nor betray one another, nor put their own little ones to work digging worms before their time. You will hear them sing while they work. The best you can do is swear and smoke."

I was gone from the eastern coal fields for eight years. Meanwhile I was busy, waging the old struggle in various fields. I went West and took part in the strike of the machinists of the Southern Pacific Railroad, the corporation that swung California by its golden tail, that controlled its legislature, its farmers, its preachers, its workers.

Then I went to Alabama. In 1904 and '05 there were great strikes in and around Birmingham. The workers of the Louisville and Nashville Railroad were on strike. Jay Gould owned the railroad and thought he owned the workers along with the ties and locomotives and rolling stock. The miners struck in sympathy. These widespread strikes were part of the American Railway Union strike, led by Eugene Debs, a railway worker.

One day the governor called Douglas Wilson, the chairman of the strike committee, to his office. He said, "You call this strike off immediately. If you don't do it, I shall."

"Governor," said Douglas, "I can't call off the strike until the men get the concessions that they struck for."

"Then I will call out the militia," said he.

"Then what in hell do you think we will be doing while you are getting the militia ready!"

The governor knew then he had a fight on, for Douglas was a heroic fighter; a fine, open character whom the governor himself respected.

The militia were called out. There was a long drawn out fight. I was forbidden to leave town without permit, forbidden to hold meetings. Nevertheless I slipped through the ranks of the soldiers without their knowing who I was—just an old woman going to a missionary meeting to knit mittens for the heathen of Africa!

I went down to Rockton, a mining camp, with William Malley and held a meeting.

Coming back on the train the conductor recognized me.

"Mother Jones," he said, "did you hold a meeting in Rockton?"

"I certainly did," said I.

He reported me to the general manager and there was hell to pay but I kept right on with my agitation. The strike dragged on. Debs was put in jail. The leaders were prosecuted. At last the strike was called off. I was in Birmingham.

Debs was on his way north after being released from jail and the local union arranged a public meeting for him. We rented the opera house and advertised the meeting widely. He was to speak Sunday evening. Sunday afternoon the committee were served with an injunction, prohibiting the meeting. The owner of the opera house was also notified that he would not be allowed to open the doors of his building.

The chairman of the committee on the meeting didn't have much fighting blood in him, so I told several of the boys to say nothing to him but go over to Bessemer and Pratt, near-by mining towns, and bring a bunch of miners back with them to meet Debs when he got off the train.

At the Union hall a large number of people had gathered to see what was going to happen.

When it was train time, I moved that everyone there go down to the depot to meet Debs.

"I think just the committee on reception should go," said the chairman, who was strong for form.

"I move that we all form a committee on reception," said I, and everybody hollered, "Yes! Yes!"

When we got down to the station there were several thousand miners there from Bessemer and Pratt.

The train pulled in and Debs got off. Those miners did not wait for the gates to open but jumped over the railing. They put him on their shoulders and marched out of the station with the crowd in line. They marched through the streets, past the railway offices, the mayor's office, the office of the chief of police. "Debs is here! Debs is here!" they shouted.

The chief of police had a change of heart. He sent word to me that the opera house was open and we could hold our meeting. The house was jammed, the aisles, the window sills, every nook and corner. The churches were empty that night, and that night the crowd heard a real sermon by a preacher whose message was one of human brotherhood.

When the railroad workers' strike ended I went down to Cottondale to get a job in the cotton mills. I wanted to see for myself if the grewsome stories of little children working in the mills were true.

I applied for a job but the manager told me he had nothing for me unless I had a family that would work also. I told the manager I was going to move my family to Cottondale but I had come on ahead to see what chances there were for getting work.

"Have you children?"

"Yes, there are six of us."

"Fine," he said. He was so enthusiastic that he went with me to find a house to rent.

"Here's a house that will do plenty," said he. The house he brought me to was a sort of two-story plank shanty. The windows were broken and the door sagged open. Its latch was broken. It had one room down stairs and unfinished loft upstairs. Through the cracks in the roof the rain had come in and rotted the flooring. Downstairs there was a big old open fireplace in front of which were holes big enough to drop a brick through.

The manager was delighted with the house.

"The wind and the cold will come through these holes," I said.

He laughed. "Oh, it will be summer soon and you will need all the air you can get."

"I don't know that this house is big enough for six of us."

"Not big enough?" he stared at me. "What you all want, a hotel?"

I took the house, promising to send for my family by the end of the month when they could get things wound up on the farm. I was given work in the factory, and there I saw the children, little children working, the most heart-rending spectacle in all life. Sometimes it seemed to me I could not look at those silent little figures; that I must go north, to the grim coal fields, to the Rocky Mountain camps, where the labor fight is at least fought by grown men.

Little girls and boys, barefooted, walked up and down between the endless rows of spindles, reaching thin little hands into the machinery to repair snapped threads. They crawled under machinery to oil it. They replaced spindles all day long, all day long; night through, night through. Tiny babies of six years old with faces of sixty did an eight-hour shift for ten cents a day. If they fell asleep, cold water was dashed in their faces, and the voice of the manager yelled above the ceaseless racket and whir of the machines.

Toddling chaps of four years old were brought to the mills to "help" the older sister or brother of ten years but their labor was not paid.

The machines, built in the north, were built low for the hands of little children.

At five-thirty in the morning, long lines of little grey children came out of the early dawn into the factory, into the maddening noise, into the lint filled rooms. Outside the birds sang and the blue sky shone. At the lunch half-hour, the children would fall to sleep over their lunch of cornbread and fat pork. They would lie on the bare floor and sleep. Sleep was their recreation, their release, as play is to the free child. The boss would come along and shake them awake. After the lunch period, the hour-in grind, the ceaseless running up and down between the whirring spindles. Babies, tiny children!

Often the little ones were afraid to go home alone in the night. Then they would sleep till sunrise on the floor. That was when the mills were running a bit slack and the all-night shift worked shorter hours. I often went home with the little ones after the day's work was done, or the night shift went off duty. They were too tired to eat. With their clothes on, they dropped on the bed . . . to sleep, to sleep . . . the one happiness these children know.

But they had Sundays, for the mill owners, and the mill folks themselves were pious. To Sunday School went the babies of the mills, there to hear how God had inspired the mill owner to come down and build the mill, so as to give His little ones work that they might develop into industrious, patriotic citizens and earn money to give to the missionaries to convert the poor unfortunate heathen Chinese.

"My six children" not arriving, the manager got suspicious of me so I left Cottondale and went to Tuscaloosa where I got work in a rope factory. This factory was run also by child labor. Here, too, were the children running up and down between spindles. The lint was heavy in the room. The machinery needed constant cleaning. The tiny, slender bodies of the little children crawled in and about under dangerous machinery, oiling and cleaning. Often their hands were crushed. A finger was snapped off.

A father of two little girls worked a loom next to the one assigned to me.

"How old are the little girls?" I asked him.

"One is six years and ten days," he said, pointing to a little girl, stoop shouldered and thin chested who was threading warp, "and that one," he pointed to a pair of thin legs like twigs, sticking out from under a rack of spindles, "that one is seven and three months."

"How long do they work?"

"From six in the evening till six come morning."

"How much do they get?"

"Ten cents a night."

"And you?"

"I get forty."

In the morning I went off shift with the little children. They stumbled out of the heated atmosphere of the mill, shaking with cold as they came outside. They passed on their way home the long grey line of little children with their dinner pails coming in for the day's shift.

They die of pneumonia, these little ones, of bronchitis and consumption. But the birth rate like the dividends is large and another little hand is ready to tie the snapped threads when a child worker dies.

I went from Tuscaloosa to Selma, Alabama, and got a job in a mill. I boarded with a woman who had a dear little girl of eleven years working in the same mill with me.

On Sunday a group of mill children were going out to the woods. They came for Maggie. She was still sleeping and her mother went into the tiny bedroom to call her.

"Get up, Maggie, the children are here for you to go to the woods."

"Oh, mother," she said, "just let me sleep; that's lots more fun. I'm so tired. I just want to sleep forever."

So her mother let her sleep.

The next day she went as usual to the mill. That evening at four o'clock they brought her home and laid her tiny body on the kitchen table. She was asleep—forever. Her hair had caught in the machinery and torn her scalp off.

At night after the day shift came off work, they came to look at their little companion. A solemn line of little folks with old, old faces, with thin round shoulders, passed before the corpse, crying. They were just little children but death to them was a familiar figure.

"Oh, Maggie," they said, "We wish you'd come back. We're so sorry you got hurted!"

I did not join them in their wish. Maggie was so tired and she just wanted to sleep forever.

I did not stay long in one place. As soon as one showed interest in or sympathy for the children, she was suspected, and laid off. Then, too, the jobs went to grown-ups that could bring children. I left Alabama for South Carolina, working in many mills.

In one mill, I got a day-shift job. On my way to work I met a woman coming home from night work. She had a tiny bundle of a baby in her arms.

"How old is the baby?"

"Three days. I just went back this morning. The boss was good and saved my place."

"When did you leave?"

"The boss was good; he let me off early the night the baby was born."

"What do you do with the baby while you work?"

"Oh, the boss is good and he lets me have a little box with a pillow in it beside the loom.

The baby sleeps there and when it cries, I nurse it.''

So this baby, like hundreds of others, listened to the whiz and whir of machinery before it came into the world. From its first weeks, it heard the incessant racket raining down upon its ears, like iron rain. It crawled upon the linty floor. It toddled between forests of spindles. In a few brief years it took its place in the line. It renounced childhood and childish things and became a man of six, a wage earner, a snuff sniffer, a personage upon whose young-old shoulders fortunes were built.

And who is responsible for this appalling child slavery? Everyone. Alabama passed a child labor law, endeavoring to some extent to protect its children. And northern capitalists from Massachusetts and Rhode Island defeated the law. Whenever a southern state attempts reform, the mill owners, who are for the most part northerners, threaten to close the mills. They reach legislatures, they send lobbies to work against child labor reform, and money, northern money for the most part, secures the nullification of reform laws through control of the courts.

The child labor reports of the period in which I made this study put the number of children under fourteen years of age working in mills as fully 25 per cent of the workers; working for a pittance, for eight, nine, ten hours a day, a night.

And mill owners declared dividends ranging from 50 per cent to 90.

"Child labor is docile," they say. "It does not strike. There are no labor troubles." Mill owners point to the lace curtains in the windows of the children's homes. To the luxuries they enjoy. "So much better than they had when as poor whites they worked on the farms!"

Cheap lace curtains are to offset the labor of children! Behind those luxuries we cannot see the little souls deadened by early labor; we cannot see the lusterless eyes in the dark circle looking out upon us. The tawdry lace curtains hang between us and the future of the child, who grows up in ignorance, body and mind and soul dwarfed, diseased.

I declare that their little lives are woven into the cotton goods they weave; that in the thread with which we sew our babies' clothes, the pure white confirmation dresses of our girls, our wedding gowns and dancing frocks, in that thread are twisted the tears and heart-ache of little children.

From the south, burdened with the terrible things I had seen, I came to New York and held several meetings to make known conditions as I had found them. I met the opposition of the press and of capital. For a long time after my southern experience, I could scarcely eat. Not alone my clothes, but my food, too, at times seemed bought with the price of the toil of children.

The funds for foreign missions, for home missions, for welfare and charity workers, for social settlement workers come in part, at least, from the dividends on the cotton mills. And the little mill child is crucified between the two thieves of its childhood; capital and ignorance.

"Of such is the kingdom of Heaven," said the great teacher. Well, if Heaven is full of undersized, round shouldered, hollow-eyed, listless, sleepy little angel children, I want to go to the other place with the bad little boys and girls.

In one mill town where I worked, I became acquainted with a mother and her three little children, all of whom worked in the mill with me. The father had died of tuberculosis and the family had run up a debt of thirty dollars for his funeral. Year in and year out they toiled to pay back to the company store the indebtedness. Penny by penny they wore down the amount. After food and rent were deducted from the scanty wages, nothing remained. They were in thralldom to the mill.

I determined to rescue them. I arranged with the station agent of the through train to have his train stop for a second on a certain night. I hired a wagon from a farmer. I bought a can of grease to grease the axles to stop their creaking. In the darkness of night, the little family and I drove to the station. We felt like escaping negro slaves and expected any moment that bloodhounds would be on our trail. The children shivered and whimpered.

Down the dark tracks came the through train. Its bright eye terrified the children. It slowed down. I lifted the two littlest children onto the platform. The mother and the oldest climbed on. Away we sped, away from the everlasting debt, away to a new town where they could start anew without the millstone about their necks.

When Pat Dolan was president of the Pittsbrugh miners' union, and there never was a better president than Pat, he got permission from the general managers of the mines for me to go through the district and solicit subscriptions for The Appeal to Reason. The managers must have thought the paper some kind of religious sheet and that I was a missionary of some sort.

Anyway, during those months, I came into intimate contact with the miners and their families. I went through every mine from Pittsburgh to Brownsville. Mining at its best is wretched work, and the life and surroundings of the miner are hard and ugly. His work is down in the black depths of the earth. He works alone in a drift. There can be little friendly companionship as there is in the

factory; as there is among men who built
bridges and houses, working together in groups.
The work is dirty. Coal dust grinds itself into
the skin, never to be removed. The miner must
stoop as he works in the drift. He becomes
bent like a gnome.

His work is utterly fatiguing. Muscles and
bones ache. His lungs breathe coal dust and
the strange, damp air of places that are never
filled with sunlight. His house is a poor make-
shift and there is little to encourage him to
make it attractive. The company owns the
ground it stands on, and the miner feels the
precariousness of his hold. Around his house
is mud and slush. Great mounds of culm, black
and sullen, surround him. His children are per-
petually grimy from play on the culm mounds.
The wife struggles with dirt, with inadequate
water supply, with small wages, with over-
crowded shacks.

The miner's wife, who in the majority of
cases, worked from childhood in the near-by
silk mills, is overburdened with child bearing.
She ages young. She knows much .illness.
Many a time I have been in a home where the
poor wife was sick in bed, the children crawling
over her, quarreling and playing in the room,
often the only warm room in the house.

I would tidy up the best I could, hush the
little ones, get them ready for school in the
morning, those that didn't go to the breakers

or to the mills, pack the lunch in the dinner bucket, bathe the poor wife and brush her hair. I saw the daily heroism of those wives.

I got to know the life of the breaker boys. The coal was hoisted to a cupola where it was ground. It then came rattling down in chutes, beside which, ladder-wise, sat little breaker boys whose job it was to pick out the slate from the coal as the black rivers flowed by. Ladders and ladders of little boys sat in the gloom of the breakers, the dust from the coal swirling continuously up in their faces. To see the slate they must bend over their task. Their shoulders were round. Their chests narrow.

A breaker boss watched the boys. He had a long stick to strike the knuckles of any lad seen neglecting his work. The fingers of the little boys bled, bled on to the coal. Their nails were out to the quick.

A labor certificate was easy to get. All one had to do was to swear to a notary for twenty-five cents that the child was the required age.

The breakerboys were not Little Lord Fauntleroys. Small chaps smoked and chewed and swore. They did men's work and they had men's ways, men's vices and men's pleasures. They fought and spit tobacco and told stories out on the culm piles of a Sunday. They joined the breaker boys' union and beat up scabs. They refused to let their little brothers and sisters go to school if the children of scabs went.

In many mines I met the trapper boys. Little chaps who open the door for the mule when it comes in for the coal and who close the door after the mule has gone out. Runners and helpers about the mine. Lads who will become miners; who will never know anything of this beautiful world, of the great wide sea, of the clean prairies, of the snow capped mountains of the vast West. Lads born in the coal, reared and buried in the coal. And his one hope, his one protection—the union.

I met a little trapper boy one day. He was so small that his dinner bucket dragged on the ground.

"How old are you, lad?" I asked him.

"Twelve," he growled as he spat tobacco on the ground.

"Say son," I said, "I'm Mother Jones. You know me, don't you? I know you told the mine foreman you were twelve, but what did you tell the union?"

He looked at me with keen, sage eyes. Life had taught him suspicion and caution.

"Oh, the union's different. I'm ten come Christmas."

"Why don't you go to school?"

"Gee," he said—though it was really something stronger—"I ain't lost no leg!" He looked proudly at his little legs.

I knew what he meant: that lads went to school when they were incapacitated by accidents.

And you scarcely blamed the children for preferring mills and mines. The schools were wretched, poorly taught, the lessons dull.

Through the ceaseless efforts of the unions, through continual agitation, we have done away with the most outstanding evils of child labor in the mines. Pennsylvania has passed better and better laws. More and more children are going to school. Better schools have come to the mining districts. We have yet a long way to go. Fourteen years of age is still too young to begin the life of the breaker boy. There is still too little joy and beauty in the miner's life but one who like myself has watched the long, long struggle knows that the end is not yet.

CHAPTER XV

MOYER, HAYWOOD AND PETTIBONE

The year 1906 I was active in the defense of Moyer, Haywood and Pettibone. I addressed meetings in their behalf and raised money to defray the expense of their trials.

Late on Saturday night, February 17th, 1906, after banks, business houses and courts had closed, the President of the Western Federation of Miners, Charles H. Moyer, was secretly arrested. William D. Haywood, the secretary of the union, and George A. Pettibone, a business agent, were arrested a short time later. All three men were kidnapped and carried into the state of Idaho where they were charged with the murder of Governor Steunenberg.

No legal steps to arrest these men, who were going about their business openly, were taken. The men designated by the governor of Idaho to take the requisitions to the Governor of Colorado had many days in which the labor men could have been legally arrested. But the police waited until Saturday night when the accused could not get in touch with banks for bail, when the courts were not open to hear habeas corpus proceedings, so that the prisoners could not have recourse to the usual legal defense and protection granted to the worst felon.

The men were taken secretly to the county jail and were not allowed to get in touch with relatives, friends or attorneys. Early Sunday morning, before five o'clock, the prisoners were driven to a siding near the Union Depot, placed in a special train, and whirled rapidly out of the state. No stops were made and the train had the right-of-way over every other train from Denver to Boise, Idaho.

The men were heavily guarded by armed men, commissioned by the Governor of Idaho, and by Adjutant General Wells, of the Colorado National Guard.

When the men arrived in Boise, they were taken to the penitentiary and placed incommunicado. Not for days did their families and friends know of their whereabouts.

Back of the arrest of the labor leaders was the labor struggle itself. Much of the labor war in Idaho had centered about the Coeur d'Alene district, a strip of country about twenty-five miles long and five wide in which were rich lead mines. The miners worked twelve hours a day in the mills and smelters and mines. in the midst of sickening, deadly fumes of arsenic. Arsenic poisons. It paralyzes arms and legs. It causes the teeth to fall out, the hair to fall off. Weird looking men worked in the mines: gaunt, their faces sunken in, their eyelashes and eyebrows off, a green aspect to their skin.

Then came the union, the Western Federation of Miners. The mine owners opposed the formation of unions with all the might of money and privilege and state. The miners fought back as savagely as they were fought. The strike was truly war with murders and assassinations, with dynamite and prisons. The mine owners brought in gunmen. The President of the Union urged the miners to arm to defend themselves, their wives and daughters. It was Hell!

In 1899 Bunker Hill Co. mine was blown up. The Governor called the troops which only made matters worse. The first troops were negroes. Men were arrested and thrown in jail without trial. One thousand men were herded in a bullpen.

One night a bomb, attached to his gate, killed Governor Steunenberg. Rewards of thousands of dollars were offered for the arrest of the murderers. That attracted the detectives. The Pinkerton Agency got busy. Eight years after the death of the governor, the labor leaders were arrested and charged with the crime of murder.

In those eight years the Western Federation of Miners had won the battle in the Coeur d'Alene district. An eight-hour day had been won. The miners had established their own stores. They had built libraries and hospitals. They had established funds for widows and orphans. Libraries took the place of saloons and hope the place of despair.

The mine owners paid spies to join the union, poor wretches who sold themselves to the slave owners for a pittance.

A poor tool of the corporations, of the detectives, a thing in the shape of a man, named Orchard, told of belonging to an inner circle of the Western Federation of Miners whose object it was to dynamite and assassinate. It was this inner circle to which the officers of the union belonged, and it was this circle, said he, that was responsible for the death, eight years before, of Governor Steunenberg.

The trial was held in Boise, Idaho. President Roosevelt called the men "undesirable citizens" before they had been given a chance to defend themselves. In the end they were acquitted and those who sought to destroy them because of their labor in behalf of toiling humanity had to seek other methods of destroying the Western Federation of Miners.

CHAPTER XVI

THE MEXICAN REVOLUTION

In 1910 I was summoned as a witness before Congress on the Mexican question. Mexico at that time was in revolution against the brutal oppression of the tyrant, Diaz.

Congressman Wilson asked me where I lived.

"I live in the United States," said I, "but I do not know exactly where. My address is wherever there is a fight against oppression. Sometimes I am in Washington, then in Pennsylvania, Arizona, Texas, Minnesota, Colorado. My address is like my shoes: it travels with me."

"No abiding place?" said the chairman.

"I abide where there is a fight against wrong."

"Were you in Douglas, Arizona, at the time of the arrest and kidnapping of Manuel Sarabia?"

"There was a strike going on the Phelps Dodge copper mines, and so I was there."

"I suggest," said congressman Wilson, "that you sit down, Mother, you will be more comfortable."

"I am accustomed to stand when talking and am uncomfortable when sitting down. It is too easy."

That brought a laugh from the committee.

"I was holding a street meeting in Douglas one Sunday night for the smelter workers. A great crowd turned out, the whole town. After the meeting a worker came running up to me and said, 'Oh Mother, there has been something horrible going on at the jail. While you were speaking, a man was taken there in an auto. He kept screaming about his liberty being taken from him but the cops choked him off.'

"I guess it's just some fellow with a jag on," said I. I gave it no further thought.

"I went to my hotel and sat with a dozen or so of those poor, unfortunate wretches in the smelters, discussing the meeting, when the editor of 'El Industrio' burst into the room very excited. He said, 'Oh Mother, they have kidnapped Sarabia, our young revolutionist.'

"Kidnapping seemed to be in the air just about that time. The Idaho affair was on. He was flushed and almost incoherent. I said, 'Sit down a moment and get cool, then tell me your story.'

"He told me while I was addressing the crowd and the back streets were empty, an automobile had driven out of the jail, had driven to the office of the paper on which Sarabia worked and he had been kidnapped; that his cries for help had been smothered, and that he was held incommunicado in the jail.

"I said to him, 'Get all the facts you can. Get them as correct as you can and immediately telegraph to the governor. Telegraph to Washington. Don't stop a moment because if you do they will murder him.'

"We telegraphed the governor and Washington that night.

"The next day I met the editor of 'El Industrio'—the paper which has since been suppressed—and he told me the horrible details. Sarabia had incurred the hatred of Diaz and the forty thieves that exploited the Mexican peons because he had called Diaz a dictator. For this he had served a year in Mexican jails. He came to the United States and continued to wage the fight for Mexico's liberation. Diaz's hate followed him across the border and finally he had been kidnapped and taken across the Mexican border at the request of the tyrant.

"I said, 'That's got to stop. The idea of any blood-thirsty pirate on a throne reaching across these lines and stamping under his feet the constitution of our United States, which our forefathers fought and bled for! If this is allowed to go on, Mexican pirates can come over the border and kidnap any one who opposes tyranny.'

"We got up a protest meeting that night. We had a hard time geting the meeting announced, for the papers all belonged to the Southern Pacific Railway or to the Copper Queen mine, and their sympathies were of course with the pirates. But we managed to circulate the news of the meeting through the town. I spoke.

"I am not very choice, you know, when the constitution of my country is violated and the liberties of the people are tramped on. I do not go into the classics. I am not praying. I told the audience that the kidnapping of Manuel Sarabia by Mexican police with the connivance of American authorities was an incident in the struggle for liberty. I put it strong.

"I went up to Phoenix to see the governor, whom I believe to belong to the type that Patrick Henry, Jefferson and Lincoln belong to. We have few of that type today. The general run of governors care more for the flesh-pots of Egypt than they do for the dinner pails of the workers. I paid my respects to the governor. The governor had ordered Captain Wheeler of the Rangers to go into Mexico and bring back young Sarabia. This was done.

Congressman Clark asked, "Was he a soldier?"

"Captain Wheeler is captain of the Rangers and a pretty fine fellow to be captain. Usually I think that men who head blood-thirsty armies, dressed up in uniforms for the killing, are not very fine men but Captain Wheeler is an exception.

"I left Arizona for the steel range in Minnesota where the steel workers were fighting the steel robbers.

Congressman Wilson said, "Mother Jones, do you know how long it was from the time Sarabia was kidnapped in Douglas, Arizona, until he was returned?"

"Eight days."

Mr. Clark inquired, "Mother Jones, who sent Captain Wheeler there: the governor or the President of the United States?"

"That I did not inquire into, so long as they brought him back."

A congressman asked me if I had been interested in the Mexican Revolution before I became interested in Sarabia.

"I have that," said I. "In 1908 I learned that there were several men in the jail in Los Angeles—Mexicans who had exposed the rule of Diaz and the plunderers of their land. They had come to Los Angeles to carry on the fight against oppression and on some trumped-up charges had been arrested by American officers more interested in carrying out the will of the oil and land interests than in securing the rights of the people. They were patriots, like Kosciuszko, Carl Schurz, Kossuth and Garibaldi and George Washington—these Mexican men in jail, fighting against a bloodier tyrant than King George against whom we revolted.

"I was not in very good health at that time but I went out and raised $4,000 that these Mexican patriots might have attorneys and stenographers and witnesses in Tombstone, Arizona, where they were to be tried before Judge Doan. They would need every defense they could get, I knew, for Judge Doan was not a very human man, and was more friendly to the copper interests than to the interests of mankind. They were tried and sentenced to serve eighteen days in the jail at Yuma but I am sure that our efforts in their behalf saved them from being turned over to the clutches of the tyrant who would have had them murdered.

"I heard that another Mexican patriot, Sylva, was apparently dying in the penitentiary in Leavenworth. I went to see him. I was angry that an American jail should imprison a man whose sole crime was his opposition to the exploitation of his people by foreign capital, that had taken over the oil and minerals and the land of Mexico. That had made the peon a slave to international finance.

"I went to see President Taft about the matter. 'Mother,' he said, 'if you will bring me the evidence in the case, I will read it over.'

"I did this, recommending to the President that he pardon the patriots that languished in our jails.

" 'Mother Jones,' said the President, 'I am very much afraid if I put the pardoning power in your hands, there would not be anyone left in the penitentiaries.'

" 'Mr. President,' said I, 'if this nation devoted half the money and energy it devotes to penitentiaries to giving men an opportunity in life, there would be fewer men to pardon out of jails.'

"As a patriotic American I never lost interest in the Mexican revolution. I believe that this country is the cradle of liberty. I believe that movements to suppress wrongs can be carried out under the protection of our flag. The Irish Fenians carried on their fight for Irish liberty here in America. Money was raised here to send to Parnell, the Irish patriot. We have given aid and comfort and a home to Russian patriots, protesting the acts of a bloody czar.

"Gentlemen, in the name of our own Revolutionary heroes, in the name of the heroes unborn, in the name of those whose statues stand silently there in Statuary Hall, I beg that this body of representatives will protect these Mexican men from the tyranny and oppression of that bloody tyrant, Diaz."

"Have you ever been in Mexico, Mother?" the chairman asked me.

"In 1901 I went with the Pan-American delegates to Mexico City, the Mexican government paying all my expenses. Then in 1911 I went again with Frank Hayes and Joseph Cannon. Madera had just been elected president after the overthrow of Diaz. I had a long audience with Francesco De la Barra, president ad interem, and with the chief justice; and also with Madera in his own home. I was most favorably impressed with Madera whose heart seemed filled with the desire to relieve the suffering in his country.

" 'Mother,' he said, 'when I go into office, you will come down and organize the workers and help them get back their land.'

"Then Madera was assassinated and Mexico went on in turmoil. Obregon got in in 1921. Under Madera, Antonio Villareal, one of the men who had been in the Los Angeles jail, was made ambassador to Spain. When he returned, fortunes had changed and he was arrested and released on a $30,000 bond. He came to New York to see me.

" 'You take the Pennsylvania railroad at four o'clock tomorrow evening and go to Washington and I will be on the same train. I will take the matter up with the government and I have no doubt that it will give you a square deal. You will not be dealing with these local pie counter holders but with the national government, the greatest government in the world.'

"The next morning we went to the Department of Justice.

" 'Won't we need a lawyer, Mother?' said Villareal.

" 'I will be the lawyer,' said I.

"I discussed his case with the attorney of the department and a full pardon was handed him. He was astonished. Later a friend of his came to me and said, 'Mother, I have a beautiful piece of land in Mexico. It produces the finest flowers and fruits. On it is the most beautiful lake. I will give it to you for what you have done for the Mexican revoluntionists.'

"I thanked him and said, 'I cannot accept compensation for doing a humane act for my fellow man. I want no strings tied to me. I want to be free to play my part in the fight for a happier civilization whether that fight is in America, Mexico, Africa or Russia.' "

CHAPTER XVII

How the Women Sang Themselves
Out of Jail

The miners in Greensburg, Pennsylvania, went on strike for more wages. Their pay was pitifully low. In answer to the cry for bread, the Irish—that is the Pennsylvania—constabulary were sent into the district.

One day a group of angry women were standing in front of the mine, hooting at the scabs that were taking the bread from their children's mouths. The sheriff came and arrested all the women "for disturbing the peace." Of course, he should have arrested the scabs, for they were the ones who really disturbed it.

I told them to take their babies and tiny children along with them when their case came up in court. They did this and while the judge was sentencing them to pay thirty dollars or serve thirty days in jail, the babies set up a terrible wail so that you could hardly hear the old judge. He scowled and asked the women if they had some one to leave the children with.

I whispered to the women to tell the judge that miners' wives didn't keep nurse girls; that God gave the children to their mothers and He held them responsible for their care.

Two mounted police were called to take the women to the jail, some ten miles away. They were put on an interurban car with two policemen to keep them from running away. The car stopped and took on some scabs. As soon as the car started the women began cleaning up the scabs. The two policemen were too nervous to do anything. The scabs, who were pretty much scratched up, begged the motorman to stop and let them off but the motorman said it was against the law to stop except at the station. That gave the women a little more time to trim the fellows. When they got to the station, those scabs looked as if they had been sleeping in the tiger cat's cage at the zoo.

When they got to Greensburg, the women sang as the car went through the town. A great crowd followed the car, singing with them. As the women, carrying their babies, got off the car before the jail the crowd cheered and cheered them. The police officers handed the prisoners over to the sheriff and both of them looked relieved.

The sheriff said to me, "Mother, I would rather you brought me a hundred men than those women. Women are fierce!"

"I didn't bring them to you, sheriff," said I, " 'twas the mining company's judge sent them to you for a present."

The sheriff took them upstairs, put them all

in a room and let me stay with them for a long while. I told the women:

"You sing the whole night long. You can spell one another if you get tired and hoarse. Sleep all day and sing all night and don't stop for anyone. Say you're singing to the babies. I will bring the little ones milk and fruit. Just you all sing and sing."

The sheriff's wife was an irritable little cat. She used to go up and try to stop them because she couldn't sleep. Then the sheriff sent for me and asked me to stop them.

"I can't stop them," said I. "They are singing to their little ones. You telephone to the judge to order them loose."

Complaints came in by the dozens: from hotels and lodging houses and private homes.

"Those women howl like cats," said a hotel keeper to me.

"That's no way to speak of women who are singing patriotic songs and lullabies to their little ones," said I.

Finally after five days in which everyone in town had been kept awake, the judge ordered their release. He was a narrow-minded, irritable, savage-looking old animal and hated to do it but no one could muzzle those women!

CHAPTER XVIII

VICTORY IN WEST VIRGINIA

One morning when I was west, working for the Southern Pacific machinists, I read in the paper that the Paint Creek Coal Company would not settle with their men and had driven them out into the mountains. I knew that Paint Creek country. I had helped the miners organize that district in 1904 and now the battle had to be fought all over again.

I cancelled all my speaking dates in California, tied up all my possessions in a black shawl—I like traveling light—and went immediately to West Virginia. I arrived in Charleston in the morning, went to a hotel, washed up and got my breakfast early in order to catch the one local train a day that goes into Paint Creek.

The train wound in and out among the mountains, dotted here and there with the desolate little cabins of miners. From the brakemen and the conductor of the train I picked up the story of the strike. It had started on the other side of the Kanawha hills in a frightful district called "Russia,"—Cabin Creek. Here the miners had been peons for years, kept in slavery by the guns of the coal company, and by the system of paying in scrip so that a miner never had any money should he wish to leave the district. He was cheated of his wages when his coal was weighed, cheated in the company store where he was forced to purchase his food, charged an exorbitant rent for his kennel in which he lived and bred, docked for school tax and burial tax and physician and for "protection," which meant the gunmen who shot him back into the mines if he rebelled or so much as murmured against his outrageous exploitation. No one was allowed in the Cabin Creek district without explaining his reason for being there to the gunmen who patrolled the roads, all of which belonged to the coal company. The miners finally struck—it was a strike of desperation.

The strike of Cabin Creek spread to Paint Creek, where the operators decided to throw their fate in with the operators of Cabin Creek. Immediately all civil and constitutional rights were suspended. The miners were told to quit their houses, and told at the point of a gun. They established a tent colony in Holly Grove and Mossey. But they were not safe here from the assaults of the gunmen, recruited in the big cities from the bums and criminals.

To protect their women and children, who were being shot with poisoned bullets, whose houses were entered and rough-housed, the miners armed themselves as did the early settlers against the attacks of wild Indians.

"Mother, it will be sure death for you to go into the Creeks," the brakeman told me. "Not an organizer dares go in there now. They have machine guns on the highway, and those gunmen don't care whom they kill."

The train stopped at Paint Creek Junction and I got off. There were a lot of gunmen, armed to the teeth, lolling about. Everything was still and no one would know of the bloody war that was raging in those silent hills, except for the sight of those guns and the strange, terrified look on everyone's face.

I stood for a moment looking up at the everlasting hills when suddenly a little boy ran screaming up to me, crying, "Oh Mother Jones! Mother Jones! Did you come to stay with us?" He was crying and rubbing his eyes with his dirty little fist.

"Yes, my lad, I've come to stay," said I.

A guard was listening.

"You have?" says he.

"I have!" says I.

The little fellow threw his arms around my knees and held me tight.

"Oh Mother, Mother," said he, "they drove my papa away and we don't know where he is, and they threw my mama and all the kids out of the house and they beat my mama and they beat me."

He started to cry again and I led him away

up the creek. All the way he sobbed out his sorrows, sorrows no little child should ever know; told of brutalities no child should ever witness.

"See, Mother, I'm all sore where the gunmen hit me," and he pulled down his cotton shirt and showed me his shoulders which were black and blue.

"The gunmen did that?"

"Yes, and my mama's worse'n that!" Suddenly he began screaming, "The gunmen! The gunmen! Mother, when I'm a man I'm going to kill twenty gunmen for hurting my mama! I'm going to kill them dead—all dead!"

I went up to the miners' camp in Holly Grove where all through the winter, through snow and ice and blizzard, men and women and little children had shuddered in canvas tents that America might be a better country to live in. I listened to their stories. I talked to Mrs. Sevilla whose unborn child had been kicked dead by gunmen while her husband was out looking for work. I talked with widows, whose husbands had been shot by the gunmen; with children whose frightened faces talked more effectively than their baby tongues. I learned how the scabs had been recruited in the cities, locked in boxcars, and delivered to the mines like so much pork.

"I think the strike is lost, Mother," said an old miner whose son had been killed.

"Lost! Not until your souls are lost!" said I.

I traveled up and down the Creek, holding meetings, rousing the tired spirits of the miners. I got three thousand armed miners to march over the hills secretly to Charleston, where we read a declaration of war to Governor Glasscock who, scared as a rabbit, met us on the steps of the state house. We gave him just twenty-four hours to get rid of the gunmen, promising him that hell would break loose if he didn't. He did. He sent the state militia in, who at least were responsible to society and not to the operators alone.

One night in July, a young man, Frank Keeney, came to me. "Mother," he said, "I have been up to Charleston trying to get some one to go up to Cabin Creek, and I can't get anyone to go. The national officers say they don't want to get killed. Boswell told me you were over here in the Paint Creek and that perhaps you might come over into the Cabin Creek district."

"I'll come up ," said I. "I've been thinking of invading that place for some time."

I knew all about Cabin Creek—old Russia. Labor organizer after organizer had been beaten into insensibility, thrown into the creek, tossed into some desolate ravine. The creek ran with the blood of brave men, of workers who had tried to escape their bondage.

"Where can we hold our meetings?" I asked.

"I don't know, Mother. The company owns every bit of dust for twenty square miles about. And the guards arrest you for trespassing."

"Is there an incorporated village anywhere near?"

"Eksdale," said he, "is free."

"Bill a meeting for me there Tuesday night. Get the railway men to circulate the bills."

Monday night, a fellow by the name of Ben Morris, a national board member came to me and said, "Mother, I understand you are going up to Cabin Creek tomorrow. Do you think that is wise?"

"It's not wise," said I, "but necessary."

"Well, if you go, I'll go," said he.

"No, I think it is better for me to go alone. You represent the National office. I don't. I'm not responsible to anyone. If anything happens and you are there, the operators might sue the Union for damages. I go as a private citizen. All they can do to me is to put me in jail. I'm used to that."

He left me and went directly to the governor and told him to send a company of the militia up to Cabin Creek as I was going up there. Then he got the sheriff to give him a body guard and he sneaked up behind me. At any rate I did not see him or the militia on the train nor did I see them when I got off.

In Eksdale a sympathetic merchant let me stay in his house until the meeting began.

When I got off the train, two or three miners met me.

"Mother," they said, "did you know there is a detective along with you. He's behind you now . . . the fellow with the red necktie.

I looked around. I went up to him.

"Isn't your name Corcoran?" said I.

"Why, yes," said he, surprised.

"Aren't you the Corcoran who followed me up New River in the strike of 1902? You were working for the Chesapeake and Ohio Railroad and the coal company then."

"Why, yes," said he, "but you know people change!"

"Not sewer rats," said I. "A sewer rat never changes!"

That night we held a meeting. When I got up to speak I saw the militia that the national organizer had had the governor send. The board member was there. He had made arrangements with the local chairman to introduce him. He began speaking to the men about being good and patient and trusting to the justice of their cause.

I rose. "Stop that silly trash," said I. I motioned him to a chair. The men hollered, "sit down! sit down!"

He sat. Then I spoke.

"You men have come over the mountains,"

said I, "twelve, sixteen miles. Your clothes are thin. Your shoes are out at the toes. Your wives and little ones are cold and hungry! You have been robbed and enslaved for years! And now Billy Sunday comes to you and tells you to be good and patient and trust to justice! What silly trash to tell to men whose goodness and patience has cried out to a deaf world."

I could see the tears in the eyes of those poor fellows. They looked up into my face as much as to say, "My God, Mother, have you brought us a ray of hope?"

Some one screamed, "Organize us, Mother!"

Then they all began shouting . . . "Organize us! Organize us!"

"March over to that dark church on the corner and I will give you the obligation," said I.

The men started marching. In the dark the spies could not identify them.

"You can't organize those men," said the board member, "because you haven't the ritual."

"The ritual, hell," said I. "I'll make one up!"

"They have to pay fifteen dollars for a charter," said he.

"I will get them their charter," said I. "Why these poor wretches haven't fifteen cents for a sandwich. All you care about is your salary regardless of the destiny of these men."

On the steps of the darkened church, I organized those men. They raised their hands and took the obligation to the Union.

"Go home from this meeting," said I. "Say nothing about being a union man. Put on your overalls in the morning, take your dinner buckets and go to work in the mines, and get the other men out."

They went to work. Every man who had attended the meeting was discharged. That caused the strike, a long, bitter, cruel strike. Bullpens came. Flags came. The militia came. More hungry, more cold, more starving, more ragged than Washington's army that fought against tyranny were the miners of the Kanawha Mountains. And just as grim. Just as heroic. Men died in those hills that others might be free.

One day a group of men came down to Eksdale from Red Warrior Camp to ask me to come up there and speak to them. Thirty-six men came down in their shirt sleeves. They brought a mule and a buggy for me to drive in with a little miner's lad for a driver. I was to drive in the creek bed as that was the only public road and I could be arrested for trespass if I took any other. The men took the shorter and easier way along the C. and O. tracks which paralleled the creek a little way above it.

Suddenly as we were bumping along I heard

a wild scream. I looked up at the tracks along which the miners were walking. I saw the men running, screaming as they went. I heard the whistle of bullets. I jumped out of the buggy and started to run up to the track. One of the boys screamed, "God! God! Mother, don't come. They'll kill . . ."

"Stand still," I called. "Stand where you are. I'm coming!"

When I climbed up onto the tracks I saw the boys huddled together, and around a little bend of the tracks, a machine gun and a group of gunmen.

"Oh Mother, don't come," they cried. "Let them kill us; not you!"

"I'm coming and no one is going to get killed," said I.

I walked up to the gunmen and put my hand over the muzzle of the gun. Then I just looked at those gunmen, very quiet, and said nothing. I nodded my head for the miners to pass.

"Take your hands off that gun, you hell-cat!" yelled a fellow called Mayfield, crouching like a tiger to spring at me.

I kept my hand on the muzzle of the gun. "Sir," said I, "my class goes into the mines. They bring out the metal that makes this gun. This is my gun! My class melt the minerals in furnaces and roll the steel. They dig the coal that feeds furnaces. My class is not fighting you, not you. They are fighting with bare fists and empty stomachs the men who rob them and deprive their children of childhood. It is the hard-earned pay of the working class that your pay comes from. They aren't fighting you.''

Several of the gunmen dropped their eyes but one fellow, this Mayfield, said, "I don't care a damn! I'm going to kill every one of them, and you, too!"

I looked him full in the face. "Young man," said I, "I want to tell you that if you shoot one bullet out of this gun at those men, if you touch one of my white hairs, that creek will run with blood, and yours will be the first to crimson it. I do not want to hear the screams of these men, nor to see the tears, nor feel the heartache of wives and little children. These boys have no guns! Let them pass!"

"So our blood is going to crimson the creek, is it!" snarled this Mayfield.

I pointed to the high hills. "Up there in the mountain I have five hundred miners. They are marching armed to the meeting I am going to address. If you start the shooting, they will finish the game."

Mayfield's lips quivered like a tiger's deprived of its flesh.

"Advance!" he said to the miners.

They came forward. I kept my hand on the gun. The miners were searched. There were no guns on them. They were allowed to pass.

I went down the side of the hill to my buggy.

The mule was chewing grass and the little lad was making a willow whistle. I drove on. That night I held my meeting.

But there weren't any five hundred armed men in the mountains. Just a few jack rabbits, perhaps, but I had scared that gang of cold blooded, hired murderers and Red Warrior camp was organized.

The miners asked me to come up to Wineberg, a camp in the Creek district. Every road belonged to the coal company. Only the bed of the creek was a public road. At that time of the year—early spring—the water in the creek was high.

I started for Wineberg accompanied by a newspaperman, named West, of the Baltimore Sun. We walked along the railroad track.

Again I met the gunmen with their revolvers and machine guns. Mayfield was there, too.

"You can't walk here!" he growled. "Private property!"

"You don't mean to say you are going to make that old lady walk that creek in that ice cold water, do you?" said the reporter.

"It's too damn good for her! She won't walk it!" he laughed.

"Won't I?" said I. I took off my shoes, rolled up my skirt and walked the creek.

At Wineberg the miners, standing in the creek and on its edges, met me. With our feet in water we held a meeting. Holding their shoes in their hands, their trousers rolled up, these men took the obligation to the union.

I was very tired. A miner stepped up to me and asked me to come to his cabin and have a dish of tea.

"Your house is on private property," yelled a gunman. "She cannot go."

"I pay rent," he protested.

"Private property, just the same. I'll arrest her for trespassing if she steps out of the creek."

The struggle went on with increasing bitterness. The militia disarmed both gunmen and miners but they were of course, on the side of the grand dukes of the region. They forbade all meetings. They suspended every civil right. They became despotic. They arrested scores of miners, tried them in military court, without jury, sentenced them to ten, fifteen years in the Moundsville prison.

I decided to call the attention of the national government to conditions in West Virginia. I borrowed one hundred dollars and went out and billed meetings in Cincinnati, Columbus, Cleveland, and from these cities I came to Washington, D. C. I had already written to Congressman W. B. Wilson, to get up a protest meeting.

The meeting was held in the armory and it was packed: senators, congressmen, secretaries, citizens. It is usual to have star orators at such meetings, who use parlor phrases. Congressman Wilson told the audience that he hoped they would not get out of patience with me, for I might use some language which Washington was not accustomed to hear.

I told the audience what things were happening in West Virginia, proceedings that were un-American. I told them about the suspension of civil liberty by the military. Of the wholesale arrests and military sentences.

"This is the seat of a great republican form of government. If such crimes against the citizens of the state of West Virginia go unrebuked by the government, I suggest that we take down the flag that stands for constitutional government, and run up a banner, saying, 'This is the flag of the money oligarchy of America!'"

The next day by twelve o'clock all the military prisoners but two were called down to the prison office and signed their own release.

From Washington I went to West Virginia to carry on my work. The day before I arrived, an operator named Quinn Morton, the sheriff of Kanawha County, Bonner Hill, deputies and guards drove an armored train with gatling guns through Holly Grove, the tent colony of the miners, while they were sleeping. Into the quiet tents of the workers the guns were fired, killing and wounding the sleepers. A man by the name of Epstaw rose and picked up a couple of children and told them to run for their lives. His feet were shot off. Women were wounded. Children screamed with terror. No one was arrested.

Three days later, a mine guard, Fred Bobbett, was killed in an altercation. Fifty strikers and their organizers were immediately arrested, and without warrant.

I went to Boomer where the organization is composed of foreigners, and I went to Long Acre, getting each local union to elect a delegate who should appeal to the governor to put a stop to the military despotism.

I met all these delegates in a church and told them how they were to address a governor. We took the train for Charleston. I thought it better for the delegates to interview the governor without me, so after cautioning them to keep cool, I went over to the hotel where they were to meet me after their interview.

As I was going along the street, a big elephant, called Dan Cunningham, grabbed me by the arm and said, "I want you!" He took me to the Roughner Hotel, and sent for a warrant for my arrest. Later I was put on the C. and O. train and taken down to Pratt and handed over to the military. They were not looking for me so they had no bullpen ready. So a Dr. Hansford and his wife took care of me and some organizers who were arrested with me. The next day I was put in solitary in a room, guarded by soldiers who paced day and night in front of my door. I could see no one. I will give the military of West Virginia credit for one thing: they are far less brutal and cold blooded than the military of Colorado.

After many weeks we were taken before the judge advocate. The court had sent two lawyers to my bullpen to defend me but I had refused to let them defend me in that military court. I refused to recognize the jurisdiction of the court, to recognize the suspension of the civil courts. My arrest and trial were unconstitutional. I told the judge advocate that this was my position. I refused to enter a plea.

I was tried for murder. Along with the others I was sentenced to serve twenty years in the state penitentiary. I was not sent to prison immediately but held for five weeks in the military camp. I did not know what they were going to do with me. My guards were nice young men, respectful and courteous with the exception of a fellow called Lafferty, and another sewer rat whose name I have not taxed my mind with.

Then from California came aid. The great, lion-hearted editor of the San Francisco Bulletin, Fremont Older, sent his wife across the continent to Washington. She had a talk with Senator Kearns. From Washington she came to see me. She got all the facts in regard to the situation from the beginning of the strike to my unconstitutional arrest and imprisonment. She wrote the story for Collier's Magazine.

She reported conditions to Senator Kearns, who immediately demanded a thorough congressional inquiry.

Some one dropped a Cincinnati Post through my prison window. It contained a story of Wall Street's efforts to hush up the inquiry. "If Wall Street gets away with this," I thought, "and the strike is broken, it means industrial bondage for long years to come in the West Virginia mines."

I decided to send a telegram, via my underground railway, to Senator Kearns. There was a hole in the floor of my prison-cabin. A rug covered the hole. I lifted the rug and rang two beer bottles against one another. A soldier who was my friend came crawling under the house to see "what was up." He had slipped me little things before, and I had given him what little I had to give—an apple, a magazine. So I gave him the telegram and told him to take it three miles up the road to another office. He said he would. "It's fine stuff, Mother," he said.

That night when he was off duty he trudged three miles up the road with the telegram. He sent it.

The next day in Washington, the matter of a congressional inquiry in the West Virginia mines came up for discussion in the Senate.

Senator Goff from Clarksburg, who had stock in the coal mines of West Virginia, got up on the floor and said that West Virginia was a place of peace until the agitators came in. "And the grandmother of agitators in this country," he went on, "is that old Mother Jones! I learn from the governor that she is not in prison at all but is only detained in a very pleasant boarding house!"

Senator Kearns rose. "I have a telegram from this old women of eighty-four in this very pleasant boarding house," said he. "I will read it."

To the astonishment of the senators and the press he then read my telegram. They had supposed the old woman's voice was in prison with her body.

"From out the military prison walls of Pratt, West Virginia, where I have walked over my eighty-fourth milestone in history, I send you the groans and tears and heartaches of men, women and children as I have heard them in this state. From out these prison walls, I plead with you for the honor of the nation, to push that investigation, and the children yet unborn will rise and call you blessed."

Then the senate took action. A senatorial commission was appointed to investigate conditions.

One hour after this decision, Captain Sherwood of the militia, a real man in every sense of the word aside from the uniform, said to me, "Mother, the governor telephoned me to bring you to Charleston at once. You have only twenty-five minutes before the train comes.''

''What does the governor want?'' said I.

''He didn't say.''

When I got to the governor's office, I had to wait some time because the governor and the mine owners were locked behind doors holding a secret conference as to how they should meet the senatorial investigation.

Governor Hatfield had succeeded Governor Glasscock, and he told me, when he finally admitted me, that he had been trying to settle the strike ever since he had been elected.

''I could have settled it in twenty-four hours,'' said I.

He shook his head mournfully.

''I would make the operators listen to the grievances of their workers. I would take the $650,000 spent for the militia during this strike and spend it on schools and playgrounds and libraries that West Virginia might have a more highly developed citizenry, physically and intellectually. You would then have fewer little children in the mines and factories; fewer later in jails and penitentiaries; fewer men and women submitting to conditions that are brutalizing and un-American.''

The next day he attended the convention of the miners that was in session in Charleston. I saw him there and I said to him, ''Governor, I am going out of town tomorrow.''

''Where are you going?''

"I'm going to consult a brain specialist. My brain got out of balance while I was in the bull-pen."

"Didn't you know I was a doctor?" said he.

"Your pills won't do me any good!" I said.

Shortly after the miner's convention, Governor Hatfield set aside all the military sentences, freeing all of the prisoners but eight. The operators recognized the union and many abuses were corrected.

The working men had much to thank Senator Kearns for. He was a great man, standing for justice and the square deal. Yet, to the shame of the workers of Indiana, when he came up for re-election they elected a man named Watson, a deadly foe of progress. I felt his defeat keenly, felt the ingratitude of the workers. It was through his influence that prison doors had opened, that unspeakable conditions were brought to light. I have felt that the disappointment of his defeat brought on his illness and ended the brave, heroic life of one of labor's few friends.

One day when I was in Washington, a man came to see me who said General Elliott had sent him to me. General Elliott was the military man who had charge of the prisoners sentenced to the penitentiary in the court martial during the strike. Never would I forget that scene on the station platform of Pratt when the men were being taken to Moundsville; the wives screaming frantically; the little children not allowed to kiss or caress their fathers. Neither the screams nor the sobs touched the stone heart of General Elliott.

And now General Elliott had sent a friend to me to ask me to give him a letter endorsing him for Congress.

"And did General Elliott send you?"

"Yes."

"Then tell the general that nothing would give me more pleasure than to give you a letter, but it would be a letter to go to hell and not to Congress!"

CHAPTER XIX

GUARDS AND GUNMEN

In the fall of 1912 I went to Eksdale, West Virginia. A strike had been going on in that section of the coal country for some time. A weary lull had come in the strike and I decided to do something to rouse the strikers and the public.

I called six trusty American men to me, told them to go up along the creeks on either side of which mining camps are located, and to notify all the miners that I wanted them in Charleston at one o'clock Tuesday afternoon; they must not bring any clubs or guns with them.

Tuesday afternoon, at a prearranged place, I met the boys in Charleston. The camps had turned out in full. I told the lads to follow me, and they did, through the streets of Charleston with a banner that said, "Nero fiddled while Rome burned." "Nero" was the governor who fiddled with the moneyed interests while the the state was going to ruin. Another banner was addressed to a certain gunman whom the workers particularly hated because of his excessive brutality. It said, "If G——— is not out of town by six o'clock he will be hanging to a telegraph pole!"

The reason that he did not hang was because he was out of town before six.

We gathered on the state house grounds. I went into the governor's office and requested him politely to come out, as there were a lot of Virginia's first families giving a lawn party outside, and they wanted him to talk to them. I could see that he wanted to come out but that he was timid.

"Mother," he said, "I can't come with you but I am not as bad as you may think."

"Come," I said, pulling him by his coattails.

He shook his head. He looked like a scared child and I felt sorry for him; a man without the courage of his emotions; a good, weak man who could not measure up to a position that took great strength of mind, a character of granite.

From a platform on the statehouse steps I read a document that we had drawn up, requesting the governor to do away with the murderous Baldwin Felts guards and gunmen. We asked him to re-establish America and American traditions in West Virginia. I called a committee to take the document into the statehouse and place it reverently on the governor's table. I then spoke to the crowd and in conclusion said, "Go home now. Keep away from the saloons. Save your money. You're going to need it."

"What will we need it for, Mother?" some one shouted.

"For guns," said I. "Go home and read the immortal Washington's words to the colonists.

He told those who were struggling for liberty against those who would not heed or hear "to buy guns."

They left the meeting peacefully and bought every gun in the hardware stores of Charleston. They took down the old hammerlocks from their cabin walls. Like the Minute Men of New England, they marched up the creeks to their homes with the grimness of the soldiers of the revolution.

The next morning alarms were ringing. The United States senate called attention to the civil war that was taking place but 350 miles from the capital. The sleepy eye of the national government looked upon West Virginia. A senatorial investigation was immediately ordered to inquire into the blight that was eating out the heart of the coal industry. Once again the public was given a chance to hear the stifled cry of the miners in their eternal struggle.

CHAPTER XX

Governor Hunt

I went into Arizona in 1913 for the Western Federation of Miners. The miners throughout the copper region were on strike. Great fortunes were being made in the war and the miners demanded their share of it. Ed Crough, a very able organizer, was with me in the field.

The strike of the miners in Arizona was one of the most remarkable strikes in the history of the American labor movement. Its peaceful character, its successful outcome, were due to that most remarkable character, Governor Hunt.

The answer of the copper kings, who for thirty years had held the copper country as despots hold their thrones, their answer to the miners' demands was to close the mines completely. The operators then left town. They built a tent colony for the faithful scabs who cared for their masters more than for their class.

Then the governor acted, acted in favor of peace. He authorized the sheriff of the copper region to deputize forty striking miners to watch the mine owners' property, to see that no violence was done to any man. He said that bullpens if built would be for gunmen as well as for any striker who advised violence. He refused to let scabs be brought in under the protection of state troops and hired thugs, as was done in Colorado.

One night during the strike I was addressing a large audience composed of citizens as well as miners.

"I am glad," said I, "to see so many union men and women tonight. In fact I know that every man and woman here is a loyal member of the union. I refer to the United States, the union of all the states. I ask then, if in union there is strength for our nation, would there not be for labor! What one state could not get alone, what one miner against a powerful corporation could not achieve, can be achieved by the union. What is a good enough principle for an American citizen ought to be good enough for the working man to follow."

The strike lasted four months, in which time there was complete lack of disorder. Though the striking miners had to go miles up the hills for their firewood, they did not touch a stick of the lumber that lay in piles about the mines, and was the property of the mine owners.

Although the bosses had gone away, leaving their houses practically open, taking nothing, when they returned they found things just as they were left.

A fire broke out in one of the mills due to defective wiring. The strikers formed a bucket brigade and put out the fire.   Two were injured.

The copper-controlled newspapers accused the miners of setting the mill on fire and in the course of their story omitted the fact that strikers saved it.   As no violence could be attributed to the strikers, the financial interests set out to "get" Governor Hunt.

In spite of their vigorous campaign of lies and fraud, Governor Hunt was chosen in the primaries and in the subsequent election.   His election was challenged.   He was counted out and a present of the governorship handed to the tool of the copper interests, Campbell.

Meanwhile the miners won their strike.   They received large increases in wages and a standing grievance committee was recognized which was to act as intermediary between the operators and the miners.

This strike demonstrated the fact that where the great vested interests do not control the state government, the voice of labor makes itself heard.   But it is hard for labor to speak above the roar of guns.

I came to know Governor Hunt, a most human and just man.   One day I saw the governor stop his machine and ask a poor man with his bundle of blankets over his back, where he was going. The man was a "blanket-stiff," a wandering worker.   His clothes were dusty.   His shoes in slithers.   He told the governor where he was going.

"Jump in," said the governor, opening the door of his machine.

The man shook his head, looking at his dusty clothes and shoes.

The governor understood. "Oh, jump in," he laughed. "I don't mind outside dirt. It's the dirt in people's hearts that counts!"

Governor Hunt never forgot that although he was governor, he was just like other folks.

With Governor Campbell in office, the bosses took heart. The miners in settling their strike with the copper kings had agreed to give up their charter in the Western Federation of Labor in return for a standing grievance committee. Thus they sold their birthright for a mess of pottage. They were without the backing of a powerful national organization. Grievances were disregarded and the men were without the machinery for forcing their consideration. Many of the promises made by the bosses were not executed.

The cost of living during the war went rocket high. Copper stock made men rich over night. But the miner, paying high prices for his food, for his living, was unpatriotic if he called attention to his grievances. He became an "emissary of the Kaiser" if he whispered his injuries. While boys died at the front and the copper miners groaned at the rear, the copper kings grew richer than the kings against whom the nation fought.

Finally the burning injustice in the hearts of the copper miners leaped into flame. On June 27, 1917, a strike was called in the Copper Queen, one of the richest mines in the world.

"The I. W. W.!" yelled the copper kings, whose pockets were. bulging. They themselves had driven out the A. F. of L., the conservative organization.

Mining stopped. Stocks suffered a drop. Wall Street yelled "German money!" No one would listen to the story of the theft of the miners' time without pay under the pressure of war; of his claim that he could not live on his wages—no one.

Guns, revolvers, machine guns came to Bisbee as they did to the front in France. Shoot them back into the mines, said the bosses.

Then on July 12th, 1,086 strikers and their sympathizers were herded at the point of guns into cattle cars in which cattle had recently been and which had not yet been cleaned out; they were herded into these box cars, especially made ready, and taken into the desert. Here they were left without food or water—men, women, children. Heads of families were there. Men who had bought Liberty Bonds that the reign of democracy might be ushered in. Lawyers who had taken a striker's case in court. Store keepers who sold groceries to strikers' wives—out on the desert, without food or water —left to die.

"I. W. W.'s" shrieked the press on the front page. On the back page it gave the rise in copper stocks.

Wrapped in the folds of the flag, these kidnapers of the workers were immune. Besides, they were Bisbee's prominent citizens.

The President sent a commission. Copper was needed for the war. Faithful workers were needed. The commission investigated conditions, investigated the frightful deportations of American citizens. It made a report wholly in favor of labor and the contentions of the workers. It called the deportations from Bisbee outrageous.

But the papers of Arizona would not print the commission's report although accepted by President Wilson.

The workers had become educated. Elections came. Again Governor Hunt was elected. The legislature had passed the infamous slave bill, "The Work or Fight Law." By this law a man who struck was automatically sent into the front line trenches. One of the first things Governor Hunt did was to veto this bill which he characterized as a "very obnoxious form of tyranny."

Out of labor's struggle in Arizona came better conditions for the workers, who must everywhere, at all times, under advantage and disadvantage work out their own salvation.

CHAPTER XXI

In Rockefeller's Prisons

I was in Washington, D. C., at the time of the great coal strike against the Rockefeller holdings in southern Colorado. Ten years previous a strike against long endured exploitation and tyranny had been brutally suppressed with guns and by starvation. But the bitterness and despair of the workers smouldered and smouldered long after the fires of open rebellion had been extinguished. Finally after a decade of endurance the live coals in the hearts of the miners leaped into a roaring fire of revolt.

One day I read in the newspaper that Governor Ammons of Colorado said that Mother Jones was not to be allowed to go into the southern field where the strike was raging.

That night I took a train and went directly to Denver. I got a room in the hotel where I usually stayed. I then went up to Union headquarters of the miners, after which I went to the station and bought my ticket and sleeper to Trinidad in the southern field.

When I returned to the hotel, a man who had registered when I did, came up to me and said, "Are you going to Trinidad, Mother Jones?"

"Of course," said I.

"Mother, I want to tell you that the governor has detectives at the hotel and railway station watching you."

"Detectives don't bother me," I told him.

"There are two detectives in the lobby, one up in the gallery, and two or three at the station, watching the gates to see who board the trains south."

I thanked him for his information. That night I went an hour or so before the coaches were brought into the station way down into the railway yards where the coaches stood ready to be coupled to the train. I went to the section house. There was an old section hand there. He held up his lantern to see me.

"Oh, Mother Jones," he said, "and is it you that's walking the ties!"

"It's myself," said I, "but I'm not walking. I have a sleeper ticket for the south and I want to know if the trains are made up yet. I want to go aboard."

"Sit here," he said, "I'll go see. I don't know." I knew he understood without any explaining why I was there.

"I wish you would tell the porter to come back with you," said I.

He went off, his light bobbing at his side. Pretty soon he returned with the porter.

"What you want, Mother?" says he.

"I want to know if the berths are made up yet?"

"Do you want to get on now, Mother?"

"Yes."

"Then yours is made up."

I showed him my tickets and he led me across the tracks.

"Mother," he said, "I know you now but later I might find it convenienter not to have the acquaintance."

"I understand," said I. "Now here's two dollars to give to the conductor. Tell him to let Mother Jones off before we get to the Santa Fe crossing. That will be early in the morning."

"I sure will," said he.

I got on board the sleeper in the yards and was asleep when the coaches pulled into the Denver station for passengers south. I was still asleep when the train pulled out of the depot.

Early in the morning the porter awakened me. "Mother," he said, "the conductor is going to stop the train for you. Be ready to hop."

When the train slowed down before we got to the crossing, the conductor came to help me off.

"Are you doing business, Mother?" said he.

"I am indeed," said I. "And did you stop the train just for me?"

"I certainly did!"

He waved to me as the train pulled away. "Goodbye, Mother."

It was very early and I walked into the little town of Trinidad and got breakfast. Down at the station a company of military were watching to see if I came into town. But no Mother Jones got off at the depot, and the company marched back to headquarters, which was just across the street from the hotel where I was staying.

I was in Trinidad three hours before they knew I was there. They telephoned the governor. They telephoned General Chase in charge of the militia. "Mother Jones is in Trinidad!" they said.

"Impossible!" said the governor. "Impossible!" said the general.

"Nevertheless, she is here!"

"We have had her well watched, the hotels and the depots," they said.

"Nevertheless, she is here!"

My arrest was ordered.

A delegation of miners came to me. "Boys," I said, "they are going to arrest me but don't make any trouble. Just let them do it."

"Mother," said they, "we aren't going to let them arrest you!"

"Yes, you will. Let them carry on their game."

While we were sitting there talking, I heard footsteps tramping up the stairs.

"Here they come," said I and we sat quietly waiting.

The door opened. It was a company of militia.

"Did you come after me, boys?" said I. They looked embarrassed.

"Pack your valise and come," said the captain.

They marched me down stairs and put me in an automobile that was waiting at the door.

The miners had followed. One of them had tears rolling down his cheeks.

"Mother," he cried, "I wish I could go for you!"

We drove to the prison first, passing cavalry and infantry and gunmen, sent by the state to subdue the miners. Orders were given to drive me to the Sisters' Hospital, a portion of which had been turned into a military prison. They put me in a small room with white plastered walls, with a cot, a chair and a table, and for nine weeks I stayed in that one room, seeing no human beings but the silent military. One stood on either side of the cell door, two stood across the hall, one at the entrance to the hall, two at the elevator entrance on my floor, two on the ground floor elevator entrance.

Outside my window a guard walked up and down, up and down day and night, day and night, his bayonet flashing in the sun.

"Lads," said I to the two silent chaps at the door, "the great Standard Oil is certainly afraid of an old woman!"

They grinned.

My meals were sent to me by the sisters.

They were not, of course, luxurious. In all those nine weeks I saw no one, received not a letter, a paper, a postal card. I saw only landscape and the bayonet flashing in the sun.

Finally, Mr. Hawkins, the attorney for the miners, was allowed to visit me. Then on Sunday, Colonel Davis came to me and said the governor wanted to see me in Denver.

The colonel and a subordinate came for me that night at nine o'clock. As we went down the hall, I noticed there was not a soldier in sight. There was none in the elevator. There was none in the entrance way. Everything was strangely silent. No one was about. A closed automobile waited us. We three got in.

"Drive the back way!" said the colonel to the chauffeur.

We drove through dark, lonely streets. The curtains of the machine were down. It was black outside and inside. It was the one time in my life that I thought my end had come; that I was to say farewell to the earth, but I made up my mind that I would put up a good fight before passing out of life!

When we reached the Santa Fe crossing I was put aboard the train. I felt great relief, for the strike had only begun and I had much to do. I went to bed and slept till we arrived in Denver. Here I was met by a monster, called General Chase, whose veins run with ice water. He started to take me to Brown Palace Hotel. I asked him if he would permit me to go to a less aristocratic hotel, to the one I usually stopped at. He consented, telling me he would escort me to the governor at nine o'clock.

I was taken before the governor that morning. The governor said to me, "I am going to turn you free but you must not go back to the strike zone!"

"Governor," I said, "I am going back."

"I think you ought to take my advice," he said, "and do what I think you ought to do."

"Governor," said I, "if Washington took instructions from such as you, we would be under King George's descendants yet! If Lincoln took instructions from you, Grant would never have gone to Gettysburg. I think I had better not take your orders."

I stayed on a week in Denver. Then I got a ticket and sleeper for Trinidad. Across the aisle from me was Reno, Rockefeller's detective. Very early in the morning, soldiers awakened me.

"Get up," they said, "and get off at the next stop!"

I got up, of course, and with the soldiers I got off at Walsenburg, fifty miles from Trinidad. The engineer and the fireman left their train when they saw the soldiers putting me off.

"What are you going to do with that old woman?" they said. "We won't run the train till we know!"

The soldiers did not reply.

"Boys," I said, "go back on your engine. Some day it will be all right."

Tears came trickling down their cheeks, and when they wiped them away, there were long, black streaks on their faces.

I was put in the cellar under the courthouse. It was a cold, terrible place, without heat, damp and dark. I slept in my clothes by day, and at night I fought great sewer rats with a beer bottle. "If I were out of this dungeon," thought I, "I would be fighting the human sewer rats anway!"

For twenty-six days I was held a military prisoner in that black hole. I would not give in. I would not leave the state. At any time, if I would do so, I could have my freedom. General Chase and his bandits thought that by keeping me in that cold cellar, I would catch the flue or pneumonia, and that would settle for them what to do with "old Mother Jones."

Colonel Berdiker, in charge of me, said, "Mother, I have never been placed in a position as painful as this. Won't you go to Denver and leave the strike field?"

"No, Colonel, I will not," said I.

The hours dragged underground. Day was perpetual twilight and night was deep night. I watched people's feet from my cellar window; miners' feet in old shoes; soldiers' feet, well shod in government leather; the shoes of women with the heels run down; the dilapidated shoes of children; barefooted boys. The children would scrooch down and wave to me but the soldiers shooed them off.

One morning when my hard bread and sloppy coffee were brought to me, Colonel Berdiker said to me, "Mother, don't eat that stuff!" After that he sent my breakfast to me—good, plain food. He was a man with a heart, who perhaps imagined his own mother imprisoned in a cellar with the sewer rats' union.

The colonel came to me one day and told me that my lawyers had obtained a habeas corpus for me and that I was to be released; that the military would give me a ticket to any place I desired.

"Colonel," said I, "I can accept nothing from men whose business it is to shoot down my class whenever they strike for decent wages. I prefer to walk."

"All right, Mother," said he, "Goodbye!"

The operators were bringing in Mexicans to work as scabs in the mines. In this operation they were protected by the military all the way from the Mexican borders. They were brought in to the strike territory without knowing the conditions, promised enormous wages and easy work. They were packed in cattle cars, in charge of company gunmen, and if when arriving, they attempted to leave, they were shot. Hundreds of these poor fellows had been lured

into the mines with promises of free land.
When they got off the trains, they were driven
like cattle into the mines by gunmen.

This was the method that broke the strike ten
years previously. And now it was the scabs of
a decade before who were striking—the docile,
contract labor of Europe.

I was sent down to El Paso to give the facts
of the Colorado strike to the Mexicans who
were herded together for the mines in that city.
I held meetings, I addressed Mexican gather-
ings, I got the story over the border. I did
everything in my power to prevent strike breakers going into the Rockefeller mines.

In January, 1914, I returned to Colorado.
When I got off the train at Trinidad, the militia
met me and ordered me back on the train. Nevertheless, I got off. They marched me to the
telegrapher's office, then they changed their
minds, and took me to the hotel where they had
their headquarters. I told them I wanted to get
my breakfast. They escorted me to the dining
room.

"Who is paying for my breakfast?" said I.

"The state," said they.

"Then as the guest of the state of Colorado
I'll order a good breakfast." And I did—all
the way from bacon to pie.

The train for Denver pulled in. The military
put me aboard it. When we reached Walsenburg, a delegation of miners met the train, sing-

ing a miner's song. They sang at the top of their lungs till the silent, old mountains seemed to prick up their ears. They swarmed into the train.

"God bless you, Mother!"

"God bless you, my boys!"

"Mother, is your coat warm enough? It's freezing cold in the hills!"

"I'm all right, my lad." The chap had no overcoat—a cheap cotton suit, and a bit of woolen rag around his neck.

Outside in the station stood the militia. One of them was a fiend. He went about swinging his gun, hitting the miners, and trying to prod them into a fight, hurling vile oaths at them. But the boys kept cool and I could hear them singing above the shriek of the whistle as the train pulled out of the depot and wound away through the hills.

From January on until the final brutal outrage—the burning of the tent colony in Ludlow —my ears wearied with the stories of brutality and suffering. My eyes ached with the misery I witnessed. My brain sickened with the knowledge of man's inhumanity to man.

It was, "Oh, Mother, my daughter has been assaulted by the soldiers—such a little girl!"

"Oh, Mother, did you hear how the soldiers entered Mrs. Hall's house, how they terrified the little children, wrecked the home, and did worse—terrible things—and just because Mr.

Hall, the undertaker, had buried two miners whom the militia had killed!"

"And, Oh Mother, did you hear how they are arresting miners for vagrancy, for loafing, and making them work in company ditches without pay, making them haul coal and clear snow up to the mines for nothing!"

"Mother, Mother, listen! A Polish fellow arrived as a strike breaker. He didn't know there was a strike. He was a big, strapping fellow. They gave him a star and a gun and told him to shoot strikers!"

"Oh, Mother, they've brought in a shipment of guns and machine guns—what's to happen to us!"

A frantic mother clutched me. "Mother Jones," she screamed, "Mother Jones, my little boy's all swollen up with the kicking and beating he got from a soldier because he said, 'Howdy, John D. feller!' 'Twas just a kid teasing, and now he's lying like dead!"

"Mother, 'tis an outrage for an adjutant general of the state to shake his fist and holler in the face of a grey-haired widow for singing a union song in her own kitchen while she washes the dishes!"

"It is all an outrage," said I. 'Tis an outrage indeed that Rockefeller should own the coal that God put in the earth for all the people. 'Tis an outrage that gunmen and soldiers are here protecting mines against workmen who ask

a bit more than a crust, a bit more than bondage! 'Tis an ocean of outrage!''

"Mother, did you hear of poor, old Colner?
He was going to the postoffice and was arrested
by the militia. They marched him down the
hill, making him carry a shovel and a pick on
his back. They told him he was to die and he
must dig his own grave. He stumbled and fell
on the road. They kicked him and he staggered
up. He begged to be allowed to go home and
kiss his wife and children goodbye.

"We'll do the kissing," laughed the soldiers.

At the place they picked out for his grave,
they measured him, and then they ordered him
to dig—two feet deeper, they told him. Old
Colner began digging while the soldiers stood
around laughing and cursing and playing craps
for his tin watch. Then Colner fell fainting into
the grave. The soldiers left him there till he
recovered by himself. There he was alone—
and he staggered back to camp, Mother, and
he isn't quite right in the head!''

I sat through long nights with sobbing widows, watching the candles about the corpse of
the husband burn down to their sockets.

"Get out and fight," I told those women.
"Fight like hell till you go to Heaven!" That
was the only way I knew to comfort them.

I nursed men back to sanity who were driven
to despair. I solicited clothes for the ragged
children, for the desperate mothers. I laid out

the dead, the martyrs of the strike. I kept the
men away from the saloons, whose licenses as
well as those of the brothels, were held by the
Rockefeller interests.

The miners armed, armed as it is permitted
every American citizen to do in defense of his
home, his family; as he is permitted to do
against invasion. The smoke of armed battle
rose from the arroyos and ravines of the Rocky
Mountains.

No one listened. No one cared. The tickers
in the offices of 26 Broadway sounded louder
than the sobs of women and children. Men in
the steam heated luxury of Broadway offices
could not feel the stinging cold of Colorado hill-
sides where families lived in tents.

Then came Ludlow and the nation heard.
Little children roasted alive make a front page
story. Dying by inches of starvation and ex-
posure does not.

On the 19th of April, 1914, machine guns,
used on the strikers in the Paint Creek strike,
were placed in position above the tent colony
of Ludlow. Major Pat Hamrock and Lieutenant K. E. Linderfelt were in charge of the militia, the majority of whom were company gunmen sworn in as soldiers.

Early in the morning soldiers approached the
colony with a demand from headquarters that
Louis Tikas, leader of the Greeks, surrender
two Italians. Tikas demanded a warrant for

their arrest. They had none. Tikas refused to surrender them. The soldiers returned to headquarters. A signal bomb was fired. Then another. Immediately the machine guns began spraying the flimsy tent colony, the only home the wretched families of the miners had, spraying it with bullets. Like iron rain, bullets fell upon men, women and children.

The women and children fled to the hills. Others tarried. The men defended their homes with their guns. All day long the firing continued. Men fell dead, their faces to the ground. Women dropped. The little Snyder boy was shot through the head, trying to save his kitten. A child carrying water to his dying mother was killed.

By five o'clock in the afternoon, the miners had no more food, nor water, nor ammunition. They had to retreat with their wives and little ones into the hills. Louis Tikas was riddled with shots while he tried to lead women and children to safety. They perished with him.

Night came. A raw wind blew down the canyons where men, women and children shivered and wept. Then a blaze lighted the sky. The soldiers, drunk with blood and with the liquor they had looted from the saloon, set fire to the tents of Ludlow with oil-soaked torches. The tents, all the poor furnishings, the clothes and bedding of the miners' families burned. Coils

of barbed wire were stuffed into the well, the
miners' only water supply.

After it was over, the wretched people crept
back to bury their dead. In a dugout under a
burned tent, the charred bodies of eleven little
children and two women were found—unrecog-
nizable. Everything lay in ruins. The wires of
bed springs writhed on the ground as if they,
too, had tried to flee the horror. Oil and fire
and guns had robbed men and women and children of their homes and slaughtered tiny babies
and defenseless women. Done by order of Lieutenant Linderfelt, a savage, brutal executor of
the will of the Colorado Fuel and Iron Company.

The strikers issued a general call to arms:
every able bodied man must shoulder a gun to
protect himself and his family from assassins,
from arson and plunder. From jungle days to
our own so-named civilization, this is a man's
inherent right. To a man they armed, throughout the whole strike district. Ludlow went on
burning in their hearts.

Everybody got busy. A delegation from
Ludlow went to see President Wilson. Among
them was Mrs. Petrucci whose three tiny babies
were crisped to death in the black hole of Ludlow. She had something to say to her President.

Immediately he sent the United States cavalry to quell the gunmen. He studied the situ-

tion, and drew up proposals for a three-year truce, binding upon miner and operator. The operators scornfully refused.

A mass meeting was called in Denver. Judge Lindsay spoke. He demanded that the operators be made to respect the laws of Colorado. That something be done immediately. It was. The Denver Real Estate Exchange appointed a committee to spit on Judge Lindsey for his espousal of the cause of the miners.

Rockefeller got busy. Writers were hired to write pamphlets which were sent broadcast to every editor in the country, bulletins. In these leaflets, it was shown how perfectly happy was the life of the miner until the agitators came; how joyous he was with the company's saloon, the company's pigstys for homes, the company's teachers and preachers and coroners. How the miners hated the state law of an eight-hour working day, begging to be allowed to work ten, twelve. How they hated the state law that they should have their own check weighman to see that they were not cheated at the tipple.

And all the while the mothers of the children who died in Ludlow were mourning their dead.

CHAPTER XXII

"You Don't Need a Vote to Raise Hell"

After the operators had refused to accept the President's terms for peace, the strike went on with its continued bitterness, suffering, patience. Strikers were killed. Gunmen were killed. John R. Lawson, an official of the Union, active in behalf of the rank and file, was arrested and charged with murder. It was an easy matter in the operator-owned state to secure a conviction. I took a train and went to Iowa to see President White.

"President Wilson said that this strike must be eventually settled by public opinion," said I. "It's about time we aroused a little. We've got to give this crime of convicting an innocent man of murder a little publicity."

"You're right, Mother," said he. "What do you think we ought to do?"

"I want to hold a series of meetings over the country and get the facts before the American people."

Our first meeting was in Kansas City. I told the great audience that packed the hall that when their coal glowed red in their fires, it was the blood of the workers, of men who went down into black holes to dig it, of women who suf-

fered and endured, of little children who knew
but a brief childhood. "You are being warmed
and made comfortable with human blood!" I
said.

In Chicago, Frank P. Walsh, Chairman of
the Industrial Commission, addressed the
meeting. Garrick Theater was crowded. He told
them of the desperate efforts of the operators
to break the spirit of the miners by jailing
their leaders.

We held meetings in Columbus and Cleveland
and finally held a mass meeting in Washington.
By this time the public opinion that President
Wilson referred to was expressing itself so that
the long-eared politicians heard.

Through the efforts of men like Ed Nockels,
labor leader of Chicago, and others, John Lawson was released on bonds. Ed Nockels is one
of the great men who give their life and talents
to the cause of the workers. Not all labor's
leaders are honest. There are men as cruel and
brutal as the capitalists in their ranks. There
is jealousy. There is ambition. The weak
envy the strong.

There was Bolton, secretary of the miners in
Trinidad, a cold-blooded man, a jealous, am-
bitious soul. When Lawson was arrested he
said, "He is just where I want him!"

I was at headquarters in Trinidad one morning when two poor wretches came in and asked
him for some coal. Their children were freez-

ing, they said.

Bolton loved power. He loved the power of giving or refusing. This time he refused. A fellow named Ulick, an organizer, was present. I said to him, "Go with these men and see what their condition is. Buy them coal and food if they need it," and I gave him money.

One of the men had walked over the hills with his shoes in tatters. The other had no overcoat and the weather was below zero. Ulick returned and told me the condition of these miners and their families was terrible.

I am not blind to the short comings of our own people, I am not unaware that leaders betray, and sell out, and play false. But this knowledge does not outweigh the fact that my class, the working class, is exploited, driven, fought back with the weapon of starvation, with guns and with venal courts whenever they strike for conditions more human, more civilized for their children, and for their children's children.

In this matter of arousing public opinion, I traveled as far as Seattle. The Central Trades Union of Seattle arranged a monster mass meeting for me. I told those fine western people the story of the struggle in their sister state. I raised a lot of hell about it and a lot of money, too, and a yell of public opinion that reached across the Rockies.

The miners of British Columbia were on

strike. They sent for me to come and address them. I went with J. G. Brown. As I was about to go on the boat, the Canadian Immigration officers asked me where I was going.

"To Victoria," I told them.

"No you're not," said an officer, "you're going to the strike zone."

"I might travel a bit," said I.

"You can't go," said he, like he was Cornwallis.

"Why?"

"I don't have to give reasons," said he as proudly as if the American Revolution had never been fought.

"You'll have to state your reasons to my uncle," said I, "and I'll be crossing before morning."

"Who is your uncle?"

"Uncle Sam's my uncle," said I. "He cleaned Hell out of you once and he'll do it again. You let down those bars. I'm going to Canada."

"You'll not put a boot in Canada," said he.

"You'll find out before night who's boss on this side the water," said I.

I returned to Labor Headquarters with Brown and we telegraphed the Emigration Department, the Labor Department and the Secretary of State at Washington. They got in touch with the Canadian Government at Ottawa. That very afternoon I got a telegram

from the Emigration Department that I might
go anywhere I wanted in Canada.

The next morning when I went to get on the
boat, the Canadian official with whom I had
spoken the day before ran and hid. He had
found out who my uncle was!

I addressed meetings in Victoria. Then I
went up to the strike zone. A regiment of
Canadian Kilties met the train, squeaking on
their bagpipes. Down the street came a delegation of miners but they did not wear cro-
cheted petticoats. They wore the badge of the
working class—the overalls. I held a tremen-
dous meeting that night and the poor boys who
had come up from the subterranean holes of
the earth to fight for a few hours of sunlight,
took courage. I brought them the sympathy of
the Colorado strikers, a sympathy and understanding that reaches across borders and fron-
tiers.

Men's hearts are cold. They are indifferent.
Not all the coal that is dug warms the world.
It remains indifferent to the lives of those who
risk their life and health down in the blackness
of the earth; who crawl through dark, choking
crevices with only a bit of lamp on their caps
to light their silent way; whose backs are bent
with toil, whose very bones ache, whose happiness is sleep, and whose peace is death.

I know the life of the miner. I have sat with
him on culm piles as he ate his lunch from his

bucket with grimy hands. I have talked with his wife as she bent over the washtub. I was talking with a miner's wife one day when we heard a distant thud. She ran to the door of the shack. Men were running and screaming. Other doors flung open. Women rushed out, drying their hands on their aprons.

An explosion!

Whose husband was killed? Whose children were fatherless?

"My God, how many mules have been killed!" was the first exclamation of the superintendent.

Dead men were brought to the surface and laid on the ground. But more men came to take their places. But mules—new mules—had to be bought. They cost the company money. But human life is cheap, far cheaper than are mules.

One hundred and nineteen men were brought out and laid on the ground. The lights in their lamps were out. The light in their eyes was gone. But their death brought about the two-shaft system whereby a man had a chance to escape in case one of the exits filled with gas or burned.

Life comes to the miners out of their deaths, and death out of their lives.

In January of 1915, I was invited to John D. Rockefeller Jr.'s office with several other labor officers. I was glad to go for I wanted to tell him what his hirelings were doing in Colorado. The publicity that had been given the terrible conditions under which his wealth was made had forced him to take some action. The union he would not recognize—never. That was his religion. But he had put forth a plan whereby the workers might elect one representative at each mine to meet with the officials in Denver and present any grievance that might arise.

So with Frank J. Hayes, Vice President of the United Mine Workers, James Lord, and Edward Doyle we went to the Rockefeller offices. He listened to our recital of conditions in Colorado and said nothing.

I told him that his plan for settling industrial disputes would not work. That it was a sham and fraud. That behind the representative of the miner was no organization so that the workers were powerless to enforce any just demand; that their demands were granted and grievances redressed still at the will of the company. That the Rockefeller plan did not give the miners a treasury, so that should they have to strike for justice, they could be starved out in a week. That it gave the workers no voice in the management of the job to which they gave their very life.

John Rockefeller is a nice young man but we went away from the office where resides the silent government of thousands upon thousands of people, we went away feeling that he could not possibly understand the aspirations of the working class. He was as alien as is one species from another; as alien as is stone from wheat.

I came to New York to raise funds for the miners' families. Although they had gone back beaten to work, their condition was pitiful. The women and children were in rags and they were hungry. I spoke to a great mass meeting in Cooper Union. I told the people after they had cheered me for ten minutes, that cheering was easy. That the side lines where it was safe, always cheered.

"The miners lost," I told them, "because they had only the constitution. The other side had bayonets. In the end, bayonets always win."

I told them how Lieutenant Howert of Walsenberg had offered me his arm when he escorted me to jail. "Madam," said he, "will you take my arm?"

"I am not a Madam," said I. "I am Mother Jones. The Government can't take my life and you can't take my arm, but you can take my suitcase."

I told the audience how I had sent a letter to John Rockefeller, Junior, telling him of conditions in the mines. I had heard he was a good young man and read the Bible, and I thought I'd take a chance. The letter came back with "Refused" written across the envelope.

Mother Jones Heading Protest Procession of Strikers at Denver

Mother Jones Doesn't Need a Vote to Raise Hell

"Well," I said, "how could I expect him to listen to an old woman when he would not listen to the President of the United States through his representative, Senator Foster."

Five hundred women got up a dinner and asked me to speak. Most of the women were crazy about women suffrage. They thought that Kingdom-come would follow the enfranchisement of women.

"You must stand for free speech in the streets," I told them.

"How can we," piped a woman, "when we haven't a vote?"

"I have never had a vote," said I, "and I have raised hell all over this country! You don't need a vote to raise hell! You need convictions and a voice!"

Some one meowed, "You're an anti!"

"I am not an anti to anything which will bring freedom to my class," said I. "But I am going to be honest with you sincere women who are working for votes for women. The women of Colorado have had the vote for two generations and the working men and women are in slavery. The state is in slavery, vassal to the Colorado Iron and Fuel Company and its subsidiary interests. A man who was present at a meeting of mine owners told me that when the trouble started in the mines, one operator proposed that women be disfranchised because here and there some woman had raised her voice in behalf of the miners. Another operator jumped to his feet and shouted, 'For God's sake! What are you talking about! If it had not been for the women's vote the miners would have beaten us long ago!' "

Some of the women gasped with horror. One or two left the room. I told the women I did not believe in women's rights nor in men's rights but in human rights. "No matter what your fight," I said, "don't be ladylike! God Almighty made women and the Rockefeller gang of thieves made the ladies. I have just fought through sixteen months of bitter warfare in Colorado. I have been up against armed mercenaries but this old woman, without a vote, and with nothing but a hatpin has scared them.

"Organized labor should organize its women along industrial lines. Politics is only the servant of industry. The plutocrats have organized their women. They keep them busy with suffrage and prohibition and charity."

CHAPTER XXIII

A WEST VIRGINIA PRISON CAMP

In July of 1919 my attention was called to the brutal conditions of the Sissonville prison Camp in Kanawha County, West Virginia. The practices of the dark ages were not unknown to that county. Feudalism and slave ownership existed in her coal camps. I found the most brutal slave ownership in the prison camp.

Officials of state and nation squawk about the dangers of bolshevism and they tolerate and promote a system that turns out bolshevists by the thousands. A bunch of hypocrites create a constabulary supposedly to stamp out dangerous "reds" but in truth the constabulary is to safeguard the interests of the exploiters of labor. The moneyed interests and their servants, the officials of county and state, howl and yammer about law and order and American ideals in order to drown out the still, small voice of the worker asking for bread.

With Mr. Mooney and Mr. Snyder, organizers, I went to the prison camp of Kanawha County where prisoners were building a county road. It was a broiling hot day.

About forty men were swinging picks and shovels; some old grey haired men were among them, some extremely young, some diseased, all broken in spirit and body. Some of them, the younger ones, were in chains. They had to drag a heavy iron ball and chain as they walked and worked. A road officer goaded them on if they lagged. He was as pitiless as the sun on their bent backs.

These were men who had received light sentences in the courts for minor offenses, but the road officer could extend the sentence for the infraction of the tiniest rule. Some men had been in the camp for a year whose sentence had been thirty days for having in their possession a pint of liquor. Another fellow told me he was bringing some whiskey to a sick man. He was arrested, given sixty days and fined $100. Unable to pay he was sentenced to five months in the prison camp, and after suffering hell's tortures he had attempted to run away. He was caught and given four additional months.

At night the miserable colony were driven to their horrible sleeping quarters. For some, there were iron cages. Iron bunks with only a thin cloth mattress over them. Six prisoners were crowded into these cages. The place was odorous with filth. Vermin crawled about.

A very young lad slept in a cell, sixteen by twenty feet practically without ventilation, with sixteen negroes, some of whom suffered from venereal disease. There was no sewage system, and the only toilet for this group was a hole in the floor of the cell with a tub beneath. It was not emptied until full. Great greedy flies buzzed about the cells and cages. They lighted on the stripped bodies of the men.

The sick had no care, no medicine. The well had no protection against the sick. None of the wretched army of derelicts had any protection against the brutality of the road overseers. A prisoner had been beaten with the pick handle by the overseer. His wounds were not dressed. Another was refused an interview with his attorney.

I knew it was useless to tell the governor about conditions as I found them. I knew he would be neither interested nor would he care. It wasn't election time.

That night I took the train from Charleston and went straight to Washington. In the morning I went to the Department of Justice. I told the Attorney General about conditions in the prison camp of Sissonville . . . . the fetid, disease-breeding cells . . . the swill given the men for food . . . . the brutal treatment. I asked him to make inquiry if there were not federal prisoners there. He promised me he would make immediate inquiry. This he did. To be sure there were no federal prisoners in the gang, but the investigation scared hell out of them, and the day after the federal agents had been there, fifteen prisoners, illegally held, were released.

The worst abuses were corrected for a while, at least.

Whenever things go wrong, I generally head for the National government with my grievances. I do not find it hard to get redress.

I do not believe that iron bars and brutal treatment have ever been cures for crime. And certainly I feel that in our great enlightened country, there is no reason for going back to the middle ages and their forms of torture for the criminal.

CHAPTER XXIV

THE STEEL STRIKE OF 1919

During the war the working people were made to believe they amounted to something. Gompers, the President of the Amerian Federation of labor, conferred with copper kings and lumber kings and coal kings, speaking for the organized workers. Up and down the land the workers heard the word, "democracy." They were asked to work for it. To give their wages to it. To give their lives for it. They were told that their labor, their money, their flesh were the bulwarks against tyranny and autocracy.

So believing, the steel workers, 300,000 of them, rose en masse against Kaiser Gary, the President of the American Steel Corporation. The slaves asked their czar for the abolition of the twelve-hour day, for a crumb from the huge loaf of profits made in the great war, and for the right to organize.

Czar Gary met his workers as is the customary way with tyrants. He could not shoot them down as did Czar Nicholas when petitioned by his peasants. But he ordered the constabulary out. He ordered forth his two faithful generals: fear and starvation, one to clutch at the worker's throat and the other at his stomach and the stomachs of his little children.

When the steel strike was being organized, I was in Seattle with Jay G. Brown, President of the Shingle Workers of America.

"We ought to go East and help organize those slaves," I said to Brown.

"They'll throw us in jail, Mother!" he said.

"Well, they're our own jails, aren't they? Our class builds them."

I came East. So did Jay G. Brown—a devoted worker for the cause of the steel slaves.

The strike in the steel industry was called in September, 1919. Gary as spokesman for the industry refused to consider any sort of appointment with his workers. What did it matter to him that thousands upon thousands of workers in Bethlehem, Pennsylvania, worked in front of scorching furnaces twelve long hours, through the day, through the night, while he visited the Holy Land where Our Lord was born in a manger!

I traveled up and down the Monongahela River. Most of the places where the steel workers were on strike meetings were forbidden. If I were to stop to talk to a woman on the street about her child, a cossack would come charging down upon us and we would have to run for our lives. If I were to talk to a man in the streets of Braddock, we would be arrested for unlawful assembly.

In the towns of Sharon and Farrell, Pennsylvania, the lick-spittle authorities forbade all assembly. The workers by the thousands marched into Ohio where the Constitution of the United States instead of the Steel Corporation's constitution was law.

I asked a Pole where he was going. I was visiting his sick wife; taking a bit of milk to her new baby. Her husband was washing his best shirt in the sink.

"Where I go? Tomorrow I go America," he said, meaning he was going on the march to Ohio.

I spoke often to the strikers. Many of them were foreigners but they knew what I said. I told them, "We are to see whether Pennsylvania belongs to Kaiser Gary or Uncle Sam. If Gary's got it, we are going to take it away from him and give it back to Uncle Sam. When we are ready we can scare and starve and lick the whole gang. Your boys went over to Europe. They were told to clean up the Kaiser. Well, they did it. And now you and your boys are going to clean up the kaisers at home. Even if they have to do it with a leg off and an arm gone, and eyes out.

"Our Kaisers sit up and smoke seventy-five cent cigars and have lackeys with knee pants bring them champagne while you starve, while you grow old at forty, stoking their furnaces. You pull in your belts while they banquet. They have stomachs two miles long and two miles wide and you fill them. Our Kaisers have stomachs of steel and hearts of steel and tears of steel for the 'poor Belgians.'

"If Gary wants to work twelve hours a day let him go in the blooming mills and work. What we want is a little leisure, time for music, playgrounds, a decent home, books, and the things that make life worth while."

I was speaking in Homestead. A group of organizers were with me in an automobile. As soon as a word was said, the speaker was immediately arrested by the steel bosses' sheriffs. I rose to speak. An officer grabbed me.

"Under arrest!" he said.

We were taken to jail. A great mob of people collected outside the prison. There was angry talk. The jailer got scared. He thought there might be lynching and he guessed who would be lynched. The mayor was in the jail, too, confering with the jailer. He was scared. He looked out of the office windows and he saw hundreds of workers milling around and heard them muttering.

The jailer came to Mr. Brown and asked him what he had better do.

"Why don't you let Mother Jones go out and speak to them," he said. "They'll do anything she says."

So the jailer came to me and asked me to speak to the boys outside and ask them to go home.

I went outside the jail and told the boys I was going to be released shortly on bond, and that they should go home now and not give any trouble. I got them in a good humor and pretty soon they went away. Meanwhile while I was speaking, the mayor had sneaked out the back way.

We were ordered to appear in the Pittsburgh court the next morning. A cranky old judge asked me if I had had a permit to speak on the streets.

"Yes, sir," said I. "I had a permit."

"Who issued it?" he growled.

"Patrick Henry; Thomas Jefferson; John Adams!" said I.

The mention of those patriots who gave us our charter of liberties made the old steel judge sore. He fined us all heavily.

During the strike I was frequently arrested. So were all the leaders. We expected that. I never knew whether I would find John Fitzpatrick and William Foster at headquarters when I went up to Pittsburgh. Hundreds of threatening letters came to them. Gunmen followed them. Their lives were in constant danger. Citizens Alliances—the little shopkeepers dependent upon the smile of the steel

companies—threatened to drive them out.
Never had a strike been led by more devoted,
able, unselfish men. Never a thought for themselves. Only for the men on strike, men striking to bring back America to America.

In Foster's office no chairs were permitted
by the authorities. That would have been con-
strued as "a meeting." Here men gathered in
silent groups, in whispering groups, to get what
word they could of the strike.

How was it going in Ohio?

How was it going in Pennsylvania?

How in the Mesaba country ?

The workers were divided from one another.
Spies working among the Ohio workers told of
the break in the strike in Pennsylvania. In
Pennsylvania, they told of the break in Ohio.
With meetings forbidden, with mails censored,
with no means of communication allowed, the
strikers could not know of the progress of their
strike. Then fear would clutch their throats.

One day two men came into Headquarters.
One of them showed his wrists. They told in
broken English of being seized by officers, taken
to a hotel room. One of them was handcuffed
for a day to a bed. His wrists swelled. He
begged the officers to release him. He writhed
in pain. They laughed and asked him if he
would go to work. Though mad with pain he
said no. At night they let him go . . . without a word, without redress.

Organizers would come in with bandages on their heads. They had been beaten. They would stop a second before the picture of Fanny Sellins, the young girl whom the constabulary had shot as she bent protectingly over some children. She had died. They had only been beaten.

Foreigners were forever rushing in with tales of violence. They did not understand. Wasn't this America? Hadn't they come to America to be free?

We could not get the story of the struggle of these slaves over to the public. The press groveled at the feet of the steel Gods. The local pulpits dared not speak. Intimidation stalked the churches, the schools, the theaters. The rule of steel was absolute.

Although the strike was sponsored by the American Federation of Labor, under instructions from the Steel Trust, the public were fed daily stories of revolution and Bolshevism and Russian gold supporting the strike.

I saw the parade in Gary. Parades were forbidden in the Steel King's own town. Some two hundred soldiers who had come back from Europe where they had fought to make America safe from tyrants, marched. They were steel workers. They had on their faded uniforms and the steel hats which protected them from German bombs. In the line of march I saw young fellows with arms gone, with crutches, with deep scars across the face—heroes they were! Workers in the cheap cotton clothes of the working class fell in behind them. Silently the thousands walked through the streets and alleys of Gary. Saying no word. With no martial music such as sent the boys into the fight with the Kaiser across the water. Marching in silence. Disbanding in silence.

The next day the newspapers carried across the country a story of "mob violence" in Gary. Then I saw another parade. Into Gary marched United States soldiers under General Wood. They brought their bayonets, their long range guns, trucks with mounted machine guns, field artillery. Then came violence. The soldiers broke up the picket line. Worse than that, they broke the ideal in the hearts of thousands of foreigners, their ideal of America. Into the blast furnace along with steel went their dream that America was a government for the people—the poor, the oppressed.

I sat in the kitchen with the wife of a steel worker. It was a tiny kitchen. Three men sat at the table playing cards on the oil cloth table cover. They sat in their under shirts and trousers. Babies crawled on the floor. Above our heads hung wet clothes.

"The worse thing about this strike, Mother, is having the men folks all home all the time.

There's no place for them to go. If they walk
out they get chased by the mounted police. If
they visit another house, the house gets raided
and the men get arrested for 'holding a meeting.' They daren't even sit on the steps. Officers chase them in. It's fierce, Mother, with
the boarders all home. When the men are
working, half of them are sleeping, and the
other half are in the mills. And I can hang my
clothes out in the yard. Now I daren't. The
guards make us stay in. They chase us out of
our own yards. It's hell, Mother, with the men
home all day and the clothes hanging around
too. And the kids are frightened. The guards
chase them in the house. That makes it worse.
The kids, and the men all home and the clothes
hanging around.''

That was another way the steel tyrants
fought their slaves. They crowded them into
their wretched kennels, piling them on top of
one another until their nerves were on edge.
Men and women and babies and children and
cooking and washing and dressing and undress-
ing. This condition wore terribly on the women.

''Mother, seems like I'm going crazy!''
women would say to me. ''I'm scared to go out
and I go crazy if I stay in with everything
lumped on top of me!''

''The men are not going back?''

When I asked the women that question they

would stop their complaints. "My man go back, I kill him!" You should see their eyes!

I went to Duquesne. Mayor Crawford, the brother of the President of the McKeesport Tin Plate Company, naturally saw the strike through steel-rimmed glasses. Jay Brown and I asked him for a permit to address the strikers.

"So you want a permit to speak in Duquesne, do you?" he grinned.

"We do that," said I, "as American citizens demanding our constitutional rights."

He laughed aloud. "Jesus Christ himself could not hold a meeting in Duquesne!" said he.

"I have no doubt of that," said I, "not while you are mayor. "You may remember, however, that He drove such men as you out of the temple!"

He laughed again. Steel makes one feel secure.

We spoke. We were arrested and taken to jail. While in my cell, a group of worthy citizens, including town officials and some preachers came to see me.

"Mother Jones," they said, "why don't you use your great gifts and your knowledge of men for something better and higher than agitating?"

"There was a man once," said I, "who had great gifts and a knowledge of men and he agitated against a powerful government that sought to make men serfs, to grind them down. He founded this nation that men might be free. He was a gentleman agitator!'

"Are you referring to George Washington?" said one of the group.

"I am so," said I. "And there was a man once who had the gift of a tender heart and he agitated against powerful men, against invested wealth, for the freedom of black men. He agitated against slavery!"

"Are you speaking of Abraham Lincoln?" said a little man who was peeking at me over another fellow's shoulder.

"I am that," said I.

"And there was a man once who walked among men, among the poor and the despised and the lowly, and he agitated against the powers of Rome, against the lickspittle Jews of the local pie counter; he agitated for the Kingdom of God!"

"Are you speaking of Jesus Christ?" said a preacher.

"I am," said I. "The agitator you nailed to a cross some centuries ago. I did not know that his name was known in the region of steel!"

They all said nothing and left.

I went in a house in Monessen where I heard a woman sobbing. "They have taken my man away and I do not know where they have taken

him!'' Two little sobbing children clung to
her gingham apron. Her tears fell on their
little heads.

"I will find out for you. Tell me what happened."

"Yesterday two men come. They open door;
not knock. They come bust in. They say 'You
husband go back to Russia. He big Bolshevik!'
I say, 'Who you?' They say, 'We big government United States. Big detect!''

"They open everything. They open trunks.
They throw everything on floor. They take
everything from old country. They say my
husband never came back. They say my husband go Russia. Perhaps first they hang him
up, they say."

"They will not hang him. Is your husband
Bolshevik?"

"No. He what you call Hunkie in America.
He got friend. Friend very good. Friend
come see him many times. Play cards. Talk
'bout damn boss. Talk 'bout damn job. Talk
just 'bout all damn things. This friend say,
'You like better Russia? Work people now got
country.'

"My husband say, 'Sure I like Russia. Russia all right. Maybe workmans got chance
there.'

"This friend say, 'You like tea?'

"My man say, 'Sure I like!'

"Pretty soon they go walk together. My man not come home. All night gone. Next day come high detect. They say my man Bolshevik. His friend say so.'"

"Have you been to the jail?"

"Yes, they say he not there. They say he been gone Russia."

"Here's five dollars," I said. "Now you take care of those little ones and I'll get your man for you."

He was in prison. I found him. Arrested by the United States Secret Service men who worked in connection with the Steel Company's private spies. Scores of workers were in jail, arrested on charges of holding radical thoughts. Holding radical thoughts and even the conservative demand for a shorter day, a better wage, the right to organize was punished with guns and prisons and torture!

He with dozens of others were later freed. With nothing against them. Five hundred "under cover" men worked in Monessen, sneaking into men's houses, into their unions, into their hearts, into their casual thoughts, sneaking and betraying. Five hundred Judas Iscariots betraying the workers for a handful of silver dollars.

With vermin like these must the worker struggle. Rather would the Steel Kings pay hundreds of thousands of dollars to these parasites than give the workers a living wage, a wage which would enable them to live as free men.

I was speaking in Mingo. There was a big crowd there. Most of them were foreigners but they would stand for hours listening to the speakers, trying to fit the English words to the feelings in their hearts. Their patient faces looked up into mine. Slag, the finely powdered dust of the steel mills, was ground into the furrows of their foreheads, into the lines about their mouths. The mark of steel was indelibly stamped upon them. They belonged to steel, branded as are cattle on the plains by their owners.

I said to them, "Steel stock has gone up. Steel profits are enormous. Steel dividends are making men rich over night. The war—your war—has made the steel lords richer than the emperors of old Rome. And their profits are not from steel alone but from your bodies with their innumerable burns; their profits are your early old age, your swollen feet, your wearied muscles. You go without warm winter clothes that Gary and his gang may go to Florida to warm their blood. You puddle steel twelve hours a day! Your children play in the muck of mud puddles while the children of the Forty Thieves take their French and dancing lessons, and have their fingernails manicured!"

As I was about to step down from the little

platform I saw the crowd in one part of the
hall milling around. Some one was trying to
pass out leaflets and an organizer was trying
to stop him. I heard the organizer say, "No
sir, that's all right but you can't do it here!
What do you want to get us in for!"

The fellow who had the leaflets insisted on
distributing them. I pushed my way over to
where the disturbance was.

"Lad," said I, "let me see one of those leaflets."

"It's about Russia, Mother," said the organizer, and you know we can't have that!"

I took a leaflet. It asked the assistance of
everyone in geting the government to lift the
blockade against Russia, as hundreds of thousands of women and little children were starving for food, and thousands were dying for
want of medicine and hospital necessities.

"What is the matter with these leaflets?"
I asked the organizer.

"Nothing, Mother, only if we allow them to
be distributed the story will go out that the
strike is engineered from Moscow. We can't
mix issues. I'm afraid to let these dodgers
circulate."

"Women and children blockaded and starving! Men, women and children dying for lack
of hospital necessities! This strike will not be
won by turning a deaf ear to suffering where-

ever it occurs. There's only one thing to be afraid of . . . of not being a man!''

The struggle for freedom went on. Went on against colossal odds. Steel was against them. And the government was against them, from the remote government at Washington down to the tiny official of the steel village. There was dissension in the ranks of labor. Ambition and prejudice played their part.

Human flesh, warm and soft and capable of being wounded, went naked up against steel; steel that is cold as old stars, and harder than death and incapable of pain. Bayonets and guns and steel rails and battle ships, bombs and bullets are made of steel. And only babies are made of flesh. More babies to grow up and work in steel, to hurl themselves against the bayonets, to know the tempered resistance of steel.

The strike was broken. Broken by the scabs brought in under the protection of the troops. Broken by breaking men's belief in the outcome of their struggle. Broken by breaking men's hearts. Broken by the press, by the government. In a little over a hundred days, the strike shivered to pieces.

The slaves went back to the furnaces, to the mills, to the heat and the roar, to the long hours —to slavery.

At headquarters men wept. I wept with

them.   A young man put his hands on my
shoulders.

"Mother," he sobbed. "It's over."

A red glare from the mills lighted the sky.
It made me think of Hell.

"Lad," said I, "It is not over. There's a
fiercer light than those hell fires over yonder!
It is the white light of freedom burning in
men's hearts!"

Back to the mills trudged the men, accepting
the terms of the despot, Gary; accepting hours
that made them old, old men at forty; that
threw them on the scrap heap, along with the
slag from the mills, at early middle age; that
made of them nothing but brutes that slept and
worked, that worked and slept. The sound of
their feet marching back into the mills was the
sound of a funeral procession, and the corpse
they followed was part of their selves. It was
their hope.

Gary and his gang celebrated the victory
with banquets and rejoicing. Three hundred
thousand workers, living below the living wage,
ate the bread of bitterness.

I say, as I said in the town of Gary, it is the
damn gang of robbers and their band of political thieves who will start the next American
Revolution; just as it was they who started this
strike. Fifty thousand American lads died on
the battle fields of Europe that the world might
be more democratic. Their buddies came home

and fought the American workingman when he protested an autocracy beyond the dream of the Kaiser. Had these same soldiers helped the steel workers, we could have given Gary, Morgan and his gang a free pass to hell. All the world's history has produced no more brutal and savage times than these, and this nation will perish if we do not change these conditions.

Christ himself would agitate against them. He would agitate against the plutocrats and hyprocrites who tell the workers to go down on their knees and get right with God. Christ, the carpenter's son, would tell them to stand up on their feet and fight for righteousness and justice on the earth.

CHAPTER XXV

Struggle and Lose: Struggle and Win

The steel strike was over. That is, the men were forced back to work. Only in bible stories can David conquer the giant Goliath. But the strike in the steel workers' hearts is not over. Back to the forges, to the great caldrons, to the ovens, to the flame and the smoke go the "hands." But their hearts and their minds are outside the high fences—fences that shut in the worker and shut out justice.

The strike is not over. Injustice boils in men's hearts as does steel in its caldron, ready to pour, white hot, in the fullness of time.

Meanwhile in Kansas, legislators, subservient to the money powers, were busy making laws. They wanted the workers to be life serfs of the old days, attached to their job, and penalized when they left or struck. Governor Allen signed the bill of slavery. The law was called by a fancy name and given a fair face. It forbade the workers striking. It made striking a punishable offense.

A coal strike was coming on. Governor Allen said Kansas should have coal even if the workers did not have justice. Coal was more

important than those who dug it. The coal
operators said so too.

Throughout Kansas, striking for better conditions, more adequate wages to meet the high
cost of living that the war had brought about,
for anything in fact, was forbidden, and he who
called a strike must go to jail.

President Howat of one of the districts of
the United Mine Workers sent for me to come
arouse the workers to a sense of their slavery.
I went about speaking on the Industrial Slave
Law, explaining to the workers just what it
meant to them to have the right to strike taken
from them by law.

President Howat was indicted and sentenced
to jail for calling a strike, a strike voted for by
the rank and file. Because he resisted the law
he was called a rebel.

In the early part of 1922, the United Mine
Workers held their convention. I attended.
Questions of wages and agreements were discussed. The operators in the central bituminous coal fields and the union officials had been
enjoined from making an agreement with one
another by Judge Anderson. Miners dig up
coal for the money kings and judges dig up
decisions and injunctions. But the judges get
better wages.

The question of whether the strike for April
1st, unless the operators signed agreements,
should be called by the Convention or left to a

vote of the rank and file, was before the assembly.

Howat and his friends wanted the Convention to set a strike date immediately—April first. The conservatives, led by president Lewis, wanted the body of miners themselves to vote on the issue.

Everyone was howling and bellowing and jumping on his feet and yelling to speak. They sounded like a lot of lunatics instead of sane men with the destiny of thousands of workers in their hands.

Although I sympathized with Howat, I felt that the National President should be obeyed. I rose and pushed my way to the platform. I stood there waiting for the men to become quiet. They did so. It was very still. I said:

"Boys stop howling like a lot of fiends and get down like men and do business: You are wasting time here; wasting time that ought to go to your families and babies. You ought to be ashamed of yourselves! Quit this noise!"

Some one called "Speech!"

"This is not the time for me to speak," I said. "It is time for you to act. Trust your president. If he fails we can go out and I will be with you and raise Hell all over the nation!"

After that the Convention got down to business and voted to leave the matter of striking to those who had to do the sacrificing: the rank and file.

The operators refused to meet the miners, broke their sworn agreement that they would do so. There was nothing to do but strike. The rank and file voted it.

In Kansas, against the law, the miners nevertheless went out. Governor Allen ordered them back, just as the slaves of old used to be ordered back into the cotton fields. Again they refused. Refused to desert their brothers and produce scab coal. The Governor called upon the soft collar fellows, the rah-rah boys from the colleges, the drug clerks and undertakers, the ex-soldiers and sailors who were out of work, waiting for their bonuses,—and these mined the coal. A lark it was for them. A day's picnic. They could afford to take the job with light heart and no conscience for it was but a brief job . . . not a lifetime to be spent under the ground. They would not pass on their shovel and lamp to their sons, so it was no matter to them that they left the job a little better for those who were to follow.

The government, under Hoover, opened up scores of scab mines. Non-union coal was dumped on the market. The miners believed that the Federal Government was against them. They set about organizing the non-union fields. I went here and there. I went to West Virginia. Thousands of dollars had been spent in that field. I went among the women in the tent colonies on the hills.

The story of coal is always the same. It is a dark story. For a second's more sunlight, men must fight like tigers. For the privilege of seeing the color of their children's eyes by the light of the sun, fathers must fight as beasts in the jungle. That life may have something of decency, something of beauty—a picture, a new dress, a bit of cheap lace fluttering in the window—for this, men who work down in the mines must struggle and lose, struggle and win.

CHAPTER XXVI

MEDIEVAL WEST VIRGINIA

I have been in West Virginia more or less for the past twenty-three years, taking part in the interminable conflicts that arose between the industrial slaves and their masters. The conflicts were always bitter. Mining is cruel work. Men are down in utter darkness hours on end. They have no life in the sun. They come up from the silence of the earth utterly wearied. Sleep and work, work and sleep. No time or strength for education, no money for books. No leisure for thought.

With the primitive tools of pick and shovel they gut out the insides of the old earth. Their shoulders are stooped from bending. Their eyes are narrowed to the tiny crevices through which they crawl. Evolution, development, is turned backward. Miners become less erect, less wide-eyed.

Like all things that live under ground, away from the sun, they become waxen. Their light is the tiny lamp in their caps. It lights up only work. It lights but a few steps ahead. Their children will follow them down into these strange chambers after they have gone down into the earth forever. Cruel is the life of the miners with the weight of the world upon their backs. And cruel are their strikes. Miners are accustomed to cruelty. They know no other law. They are like primitive men struggling in his ferocious jungle—for himself, for his children, for the race of men.

The miners of Logan County were again on strike in 1923. I was with them. The jails were full of strikers, with innocent men who protested the conditions of their lives. Many of them had been months in jails. Their wives and little children were in dire want.

"Can't you do something for us, Mother," they pleaded.

A delegation of their wretched wives and half-starved children came to me. "For God's sake, Mother, can't you do something for us!"

I took the train for Charleston and went to see Governor Morgan. He received me courteously.

"Governor," I said, "listen—do you hear anything?"

He listened a moment. "No, Mother Jones, I do not."

"I do," said I. "I hear women and little boys and girls sobbing at night. Their fathers are in jail. The wives and children are crying for food."

"I will investigate," said he. He looked me straight in the eye and I knew he would keep his promise.

Shortly afterward I received a letter from the Governor, telling me that all the prisoners were released but three.

For myself I always found Governor Morgan most approachable. The human appeal always reached him. I remember a poor woman coming to see me one day. Her husband had been blacklisted in the mines and he dared not return to his home. The woman was weak from lack of food, too weak to work. I took her to the Governor. He gave her twenty dollars. He arranged for her husband to return, promising him executive protection.

I was with the Governor's secretary one day when a committee called to see the Governor. The committee was composed of lick-spittles of the mine owners. They requested that the Governor put "The Federationist," a labor weekly, out of business. The Governor said, "Gentlemen, the constitution guarantees the right of free speech and free press. I shall not go on record as interfering with either as long as the constitution lives."

The committee slunk out of the office.

I think that Governor Morgan is the only governor in the twenty-three years I was in West Virginia who refused to comply with the requests of the dominant money interests. To a man of that type I wish to pay my respects.

There is never peace in West Virginia because there is never justice. Injunctions and guns, like morphia, produce a temporary quiet. Then the pain, agonizing and more severe, comes again. So it is with West Virginia. The strike was broken. But the next year, the miners gathered their breath for another struggle. Sometimes they lost their battle through their own crooked leaders. And once it was my duty to go before the rank and file and expose their leaders who would betray them. And when my boys understood, West Virginia's climate wasn't healthy for them.

Medieval West Virginia! With its tent colonies on the bleak hills! With its grim men and women! When I get to the other side, I shall tell God Almighty about West Virginia!

CHAPTER XXVII

PROGRESS IN SPITE OF LEADERS

Other strikes come to my mind, strikes of less fire and flame and hence attracting less national notice. The papers proclaimed to stockholders and investors that there was peace, and there was no peace. The garment workers struck and won. In Roosevelt, New Jersey, the workingmen in the fertilizing plant of Williams and Clark struck.

Two strikers were shot dead—shot in the back by the hired gunmen. The guards were arraigned, let out on bail, and reported back on the job. The strikers were assembled in a vacant lot. Guards shot into their midst, firing low and filling the legs of the workers with bullets.

"Mother," the strikers wrote to me, "come help us with our women!"

I went. "Women," said I, "see that your husbands use no fire arms or violence no matter what the provocation. Don't let your husbands scab. Help them stand firm and above all keep them from the saloons. No strike was ever won that did not have the support of the womenfolk."

The street car men struck along in 1916 in New York City.

I spoke to a mass meeting of carmen's wives and we certainly had those women fighting like wildcats. They threatened me with jail and I told the police I could raise as much hell in jail as out. The police said if anyone was killed I should be held responsible and hanged.

"If they want to hang me, let them," I said. "And on the scaffold I will shout 'Freedom for the working class!' And when I meet God Almighty I will tell him to damn my accusers and the accusers of the working class, the people who tend and develop and beautify His world."

The last years of my life have seen fewer and fewer strikes. Both employer and employee have become wiser. Both have learned the value of compromise. Both sides have learned that they gain when they get together and talk things out in reason rather than standing apart, slinging bricks, angry words and bullets. The railway brotherhoods have learned that lesson. Strikes are costly. Fighting them is costly.

All the average human being asks is something he can call home; a family that is fed and warm; and now and then a little happiness; once in a long while an extravagance.

"I am not a suffragist nor do I believe in "careers" for women, especially a "career" in factory and mill where most working women have their "careers." A great responsibility

rests upon woman—the training of the children
This is her most beautiful task. If men earned
money enough, it would not be necessary for
women to neglect their homes and their little
ones to add to the family's income.

The last years of my life have seen long
stretches of industrial peace. Occasionally has
come war. I regretted that illness kept me
from helping the railway shopmen in their
brave fight for recognition a few years ago.
And I rejoiced to see the formation of a third
political party—a Farmer-Labor Party. Too
long has labor been subservient to the old be-
trayers, politicians and crooked labor leaders.

I had passed my ninety-third milestone when
I attended the convention of the Farmer-Labor
Party and addressed the assembly. "The pro-
ducer, not the meek, shall inherit the earth,"
I told them. "Not today perhaps, nor tomorrow, but over the rim of the years my old eyes
can see the coming of another day."

I was ninety-one years old when I attended
the Pan-American Federation of labor held in
Mexico City in 1921. This convention was
called to promote a better understanding between the workers of America, Mexico and
Central America. Gompers attended as did a
number of the American leaders.

I spoke to the convention. I told them that
a convention such as this Pan-American Convention of labor was the beginning of a new

day, a day when the workers of the world would
know no other boundaries other than those between the exploiter and the exploited. Soviet
Russia, I said, had dared to challenge the old
order, had handed the earth over to those who
toiled upon it, and the capitalists of the world
were quaking in their scab-made shoes. I told
them of the national farce of prohibition in
America.

"Prohibition came," said I, "through a combination of business men who wanted to get
more out of their workers, together with a lot
of preachers and a group of damn cats who
threw fits when they saw a workingman buy a
bottle of beer but saw no reason to bristle when
they and their women and little children suffered under the curse of low wages and crush-
ing hours of toil.

"Prohibition," said I, "has taken away the
workingman's beer, has closed the saloon which
was his only club. The rich guzzle as they ever
did. Prohibition is not for them. They have
their clubs which are sacred and immune from
interference. The only club the workingman
has is the policeman's. He has that when he
strikes."

I visited the coal mines of Coalhulia and saw
that the life of the miner is the same where-
ever coal is dug and capital flies its black flag.

As I look back over the long, long years, I
see that in all movements for the bettering of

men's lives, it is the pioneers who bear most of the suffering. When these movements become established, when they become popular, others reap the benefits. Thus it has been with the labor movement.

The early days of the labor movement produced great men. They differed greatly from the modern labor leader. These early leaders sought no publicity, they were single minded, not interested in their own glory nor their own financial advancement. They did not serve labor for pay. They made great sacrifices that the future might be a bit brighter for their fellow workers.

I remember John Siney, a miner. Holloran, a miner. James, a miner. Robert Watchorn, the first and most able secretary that the miners of this country ever had. These men gave their lives that others might live. They died in want.

Dick Williams, McLaughlan, Travlick, Roy, Stevens, Wright, Powderly, Martin Irons, Davis, Richards, Griffith, Thomas and Morgan were pioneers worthy of our memory.

Powderly had to get up a subscription to defray the expenses of Griffith's funeral. Many of these pioneers died without even the gratitude of those whom they served. Their monuments are the good they did.

Many of our modern leaders of labor have wandered far from the thorny path of these

early crusaders. Never in the early days of
the labor struggle would you find leaders
wining and dining with the aristocracy; nor did
their wives strut about like diamond-bedecked
peacocks; nor were they attended by humili-
ated, cringing colored servants.

The wives of these early leaders took in
washing to make ends meet. Their children
picked and sold berries. The women shared
the heroism, the privation of their husbands.

In those days labor's representatives did
not sit on velvet chairs in conference with
labor's oppressors; they did not dine in fashionable hotels with the representatives of the
top capitalists, such as the Civic Federation.
They did not ride in Pullmans nor make trips
to Europe.

The rank and file have let their servants become their masters and dictators. The workers have now to fight not alone their exploiters
but likewise their own leaders, who often betray
them, who sell them out, who put their own advancement ahead of that of the working masses,
who make of the rank and file political pawns.

Provision should be made in all union con-
stitutions for the recall of leaders. Big salaries
should not be paid. Career hunters should be
driven out, as well as leaders who use labor
for political ends. These types are menaces
to the advancement of labor.

In big strikes I have known, the men lay in

prison while the leaders got out on bail and drew high salaries all the time. The leaders did not suffer. They never missed a meal. Some men make a profession out of labor and get rich thereby. John Mitchell left to his heirs a fortune, and his political friends are using the labor movement to gather funds to erect a monument to his memory, to a name that should be forgotten.

In spite of oppressors, in spite of false leaders, in spite of labor's own lack of understanding of its needs, the cause of the worker continues onward. Slowly his hours are shortened, giving him leisure to read and to think. Slowly his standard of living rises to include some of the good and beautiful things of the world. Slowly the cause of his children becomes the cause of all. His boy is taken from the breaker, his girl from the mill. Slowly those who create the wealth of the world are permitted to share it. The future is in labor's strong, rough hands.